BLAKE STUDIES

BLAKE
STUDIES

NOTES ON HIS LIFE AND WORKS
IN SEVENTEEN CHAPTERS

BY

GEOFFREY KEYNES

HASKELL HOUSE PUBLISHERS Ltd.
Publishers of Scarce Scholarly Books
NEW YORK. N. Y. 10012
1971

First Published 1949

HASKELL HOUSE PUBLISHERS Lᴛᴅ.

Publishers of Scarce Scholarly Books

280 LAFAYETTE STREET

NEW YORK. N. Y. 10012

Library of Congress Catalog Card Number: 79-117995

Standard Book Number 8383-1050-8

Printed in the United States of America

CONTENTS

v

LIST OF ILLUSTRATIONS

(A) LINE BLOCKS IN THE TEXT

(B) ELECTROTYPES OF ORIGINAL PLATES
(*Chapter X*)

(C) REPRODUCTIONS IN COLLOTYPE
(*At the end of the book*)

LIST OF ILLUSTRATIONS

LIST OF ILLUSTRATIONS

LIST OF ILLUSTRATIONS

PREFACE

Books on William Blake have become fashionable in recent years and their value has usually borne a definite relation to the amount of study expended by the author on his subject. The climax has been seen recently in the magnificent interpretative study of Blake written by Northrop Frye in Canada and published by Princeton University. Yet among all the accumulated Blake literature there are still only two books that can claim the dignity of being accorded the title of Biography—the pioneer and classical work by Alexander Gilchrist first printed in 1863 (and more recently for the million in Dent's Everyman Library), and the authoritative biography by Mona Wilson published in 1927, and reprinted last year (1948). The present volume makes no claim to a place in the interpretative series. It is rather to be regarded as an appendix, or a collection of appendixes, to Gilchrist and Mona Wilson, furnishing an elaboration of incidents or episodes in Blake's life, too detailed, perhaps, for inclusion in a balanced biography, with an occasional contribution to textual criticism and the canon of Blake's writings. There is also an obvious bibliographical thread running through the whole book, deriving from the basis on which my work on Blake began forty years ago. My interest in Blake started with the sudden conviction that the *Illustrations of the Book of Job* formed the greatest work of creative genius that my awakening consciousness had, at the age of twenty, yet recognized. Then, when

PREFACE

Gilchrist's *Life* had been read and re-read, it was borne in upon my mind that there was no adequate bibliographical substructure for the further study either of Blake's life or of his works, whether written or pictorial. This led to the compilation of the monumental *Bibliography of Blake*, published by the Grolier Club of New York in 1921 (for the volume is monumental in size, if not in content), and so in logical sequence to my edition of the complete writings (1925), and to Mona Wilson's biography, both published by the Nonesuch Press.

Some of the themes of these collected papers may seem relatively trivial, but something of novelty will be found in most of them, and in my opinion no apology is necessary for the attempt to elucidate any incident in the life of a man such as Blake, who lived his life, both corporeal and mental, with an intensity far surpassing that of ordinary human beings.

The reproductions, for which the publisher has made generous allowance, have not all been selected from among Blake's masterpieces, most of which may be seen elsewhere, but have been chosen primarily to illustrate the text, and their interest in the present context will often be found to exceed their intrinsic merit. For technical reasons connected with the present-day difficulties in book-production they have been gathered together at the end, instead of being scattered through the volume as convention demands. A section of the volume thus becomes a picture-book, a feature not without advantage to the more casual observer, who may so be tempted to pursue his study of Blake into the text.

I am grateful to The Times Publishing Company for permission to reprint many of the papers which have appeared in the columns of *The Times Literary Supplement*, and to the Pierpont Morgan Library, the Fogg Art Museum, the Limited

PREFACE

Editions Club, and the Charles Lamb Society for permission
to print others. None of the papers is here reproduced exactly
as it first appeared; all have been revised and most of them
extended.

My obligations to individual friends are too numerous to
mention—but to none are they greater than to Joseph Wicksteed, whose revealing book on *Blake's Vision of the Book of
Job*, first published in 1910, helped so much to confirm and
extend my budding interest in Blake's mind and art.

GEOFFREY KEYNES

LONDON, *October* 1948

BLAKE STUDIES

I

WILLIAM AND ROBERT

WILLIAM BLAKE, son of James Blake, hosier, and Catherine, his wife, was the second son in a family of five. His elder brother, James, succeeded to the hosiery business after their father's death in 1784. James was a man of a frugal and unadventurous mind and, as far as the evidence goes, seems to have played little part in William's life, although a long letter written to him during William's stay at Felpham in 1803 suggests that their relations may have been closer than the absence of other documentary evidence has been taken to indicate. The third son, John, was referred to by Blake in a verse letter written to Thomas Butts in November 1802, as—

> . . . my brother John, the evil one,
> In a black cloud making his mone,

and is stated by Frederick Tatham to have been a dissolute youth, who "lived a few reckless days, enlisted as a soldier, and died'.[1] William's only sister, Catherine, was the youngest of the family. She lived in his house for a time, but this led to troubles between her and Mrs. Blake, so that the relations of brother and sister were not altogether happy. It was the fourth son, baptized according to the registers of the Church of St. James, Westminster,[2] as Richard, though always known as Robert or Bob,

---

[1] Tatham's Life of Blake, in *Letters* (ed. Russell, London, 1906), p. 3.
[2] Symons, *William Blake* (London, 1907), p. 22.

B

who was the only member of the family to play an important part in William's life. He was born on June 19, 1762, and so was four years and five months younger than William. Tatham's account of him verges on the over-sentimental: "Robert, the youngest son", he wrote, "was the affectionate companion of William; they sympathised in their pursuits and sentiments; like plants, planted side by side by a stream, they grew together and entwined the luxuriant tendrils of their expanding minds. They associated and excelled together, and, like all true lovers, delighted in and enhanced each other's beauties. . . . Robert was of amiable and docile temper, and of a tender and affectionate mind, and like many of those who appear born for early death, his short life was but as the narrow porch to his eternal lot; he died of consumption at twenty-four years of age." [1]

Further details of Robert's brief existence are supplied by Blake's other biographers. After the death of James Blake, senior, in 1784, Robert lived with William and his wife at 27 Broad Street, Golden Square, next door to the hosiery business, and became his brother's pupil in drawing and engraving. For two and a half years they remained in happy intimacy which was not seriously disturbed by an incident such as that related by Gilchrist.[2] "One day a dispute arose between Robert and Mrs. Blake. She, in the heat of discussion, used words to him his brother (though a husband too) thought unwarrantable. A silent witness thus far, he could now bear it no longer, but with characteristic impetuosity—when stirred—rose and said to her: 'Kneel down and beg Robert's pardon directly, or you never see my face again!' A heavy threat, uttered in tones which from

---

[1] Tatham, *loc. cit.* p. 3.

[2] Gilchrist's *Life of Blake* (ed. Todd, London, 1942), pp. 50-51. The source of the anecdote is not recorded.

WILLIAM AND ROBERT

Blake, unmistakably showed it was *meant*. She, poor thing! 'thought it very hard', as she would afterwards tell, to beg her brother-in-law's pardon when she was not in fault! But being a duteous, devoted wife, though by nature nowise tame or dull of spirit, she *did* kneel and meekly murmur: 'Robert, I beg your pardon, I am in the wrong.' 'Young woman, you lie!' abruptly retorted he: '*I* am in the wrong!' "

Early in 1787 Robert became seriously ill and soon afterwards died, being buried in Bunhill Fields on February 11. He was nursed by his brother so assiduously that William is said to have gone without sleep for a fortnight, his exhaustion being such that after Robert's death he slept continuously for three days and nights. At the moment of Robert's death he " beheld the released spirit ascend heavenward ... clapping its hands for joy".[1] Many years later, in 1800, Blake wrote to his friend, William Hayley: "Thirteen years ago I lost a brother, and with his spirit I converse daily and hourly in the spirit, and see him in my remembrance, in the regions of my imagination. I hear his advice, and even now write from his dictate." [2] It is also related by John Thomas Smith, who had been one of Robert's playfellows as a boy, in illustration of Blake's power of disuniting all other thoughts from his mind whenever he wished to indulge in thinking of any particular subject (or person, he might have added), that "after deeply perplexing himself as to the mode of accomplishing the publication of his illustrated songs, without their being subject to the expense of letter-press, his brother Robert stood before him in one of his visionary imaginations, and so decidedly directed him in the way in which he ought to proceed, that he immediately followed his advice,

[1] Gilchrist, *loc cit.* p. 51.
[2] *Poetry and Prose* (ed. Keynes, London, 1939), p. 838.

5

by writing his poetry, and drawing his marginal subjects of embellishments in outline upon the copperplate with an impervious liquid, and then eating the plain parts or lights away with *aqua fortis* considerably below them, so that the outlines were left as a stereotype." [1] I have pointed out on another page that the process is likely to have been first brought to Blake's notice as early as 1784, when his friend George Cumberland published an account of it in Maty's *New Review*. Nevertheless it is no doubt true that Blake's visionary mind was often filled with memories of his beloved brother and with such characteristic intensity that Robert's very presence seemed to be before him and to speak into his ears. In Blake's long poem, *Milton*, written and etched on copper in the years 1800 to 1808, are two plates representing symbolical naked figures, one being the mirror image of the other, which are marked respectively "William" and "Robert". In either picture Milton, or Inspiration, in the form of a falling star, is entering the left foot of William and the right foot of Robert, thus illustrating many years after Robert's death William's lasting sense of their community of spirit. The left and right symbolism of the feet denotes the living William and the spiritual Robert.

Evidence enough has already been given to make clear the depth of the feeling which Blake entertained for his young brother. Intrinsically Robert Blake can have no great interest for posterity. Even if he had qualities that might have brought him to some degree of eminence, his early death prevented their flowering. Yet the reflected importance given him by his place in the life of William Blake make it worth while to put on record every particular of him that can be gathered. It is even probable that we possess a representation of his appearance traced by his

[1] Smith's *Nollekens and his Times* (London, 1828), ii, 461.

brother's hand. In the Print Room of the British Museum is a careful pencil drawing by Blake of a nude youth posed as a model (Plate 1). The subject is a well-built boy of about sixteen or seventeen years standing sideways to the spectator with his hand resting on a mantelpiece or shelf. His rounded face is turned towards the observer and his aspect agrees well with the amiable character ascribed to Robert Blake by Tatham and J. T. Smith. This drawing was reproduced in my *Pencil Drawings of William Blake* (Nonesuch Press, 1927), and I then suggested that the subject may have been Robert. I have seen no reason since then to alter my opinion that the truth of this conjecture is exceedingly probable. No other drawing by Blake from a living model is known to exist, and if he made any it seems likely that he did not keep them. A drawing of his brother would, however, be of enough importance to Blake to warrant its being preserved with the other drawings in his portfolio. Other subjects associated with Robert were, as we shall see, carefully kept and have survived to the present day, so that our picture of him can be further elaborated.

A relic of great interest has recently come to my notice, and is now described for the first time. It is a folio sketch-book possessed by Robert when he was fifteen, and its pages are filled with the evidences of William's assiduous efforts to teach him the elements of drawing. On the front cover is inscribed in large letters "Robert Blake's Book 1777" and on the inside, mixed up with a sketch of a woman's head, "Robt Blake". Again, on the back cover is written "Blake" in large Gothic characters at the top, "Robertus" in the centre, and "R. Blake" at the bottom, so that little doubt can remain as to the ownership of the book. William Blake's method of teaching his brother was to make a drawing of some part of the human body or of a whole figure to one side of a page, in order that Robert might make a copy alongside. Thus on the first page are no less than forty-one drawings of the lips and eight of the nose, the lips progressing from a few elementary lines to a full Cupid's bow. On the second page are more noses and lips together with an eye, on the third hands and arms, on the fourth a leg of Michelangelesque proportions, on the fifth faces and grotesques in profile, on the sixth and seventh full faces, on the eighth more lips and eyes, on the ninth dogs' heads and human ears, on the tenth a woman's head, the hips and legs of a kneeling figure, and a very vigorously drawn heraldic eagle—though this is in the centre and was not copied by the pupil. By the eleventh page Robert had arrived at copying the outline of the whole human figure, with vertical and horizontal lines drawn to indicate the proper proportions of the parts. At the bottom of the page are excellent sketches of a seated woman, a male torso and a small Hercules. On page 12 is a simple drawing of a woman in the dress of the period, and a head in a voluminous bonnet. It is not necessary to describe the contents of the whole volume in detail, 38 pages in all being occupied by these drawings, several of which occupy a full page and were not copied by Robert. At the beginning Robert's copies are feeble puerilities; later he begins to catch something of the spirit of his brother's style: the older draughtsman was himself barely twenty years old, and was still in his artistic infancy, though many of his drawings, bearing the authentic stamp of his later mastery, form a most valuable record of his beginnings as an artist (Plate 2).

The sketch-book contains in all 56 pages. A few are blank, and some towards the end have coloured drawings of birds and animals evidently copied by Robert from some book on natural history. Several of these are dated 1778, so that the whole book

may be regarded as the workshop of the boy who posed as
William Blake's model for the drawing now in the British
Museum—if the conjectural identification be accepted. The
book's history is partly recorded in a note written by a nine-
teenth-century owner inside the front cover. It is there stated
that it was "purchased some years since among the collection of
Thomas Stothard, R.A., at one period a personal friend of the
brother's". It is possible that the sketch-book passed into
Stothard's possession soon after Robert's death, being given to
him as a memento of the young man that he had known and
loved, for Stothard had been one of William's first professional
acquaintances and they may have worked together as draughtsman and engraver respectively as early as 1779. He may therefore have associated with Robert for at least eight years. It was
not until 1809 that Blake parted company with Stothard through
their quarrel over their rival designs of "The Canterbury Pilgrims", the story of which is well known. Stothard died in 1834,
and his collections were sold at Christie's in June of the same
year. The sketch-book was afterwards in the possession of Sir
Alexander Spearman, being sold with his books at Puttick and
Simpson's rooms on January 9, 1878. Its further history is not
known until it appeared with the property of George S. Hellman
at the Anderson Galleries, New York (lot 51) on November 25,
1919. It was then acquired for the H. E. Huntington Library,
California, and was included in the Blake exhibition held at the
Grolier Club of New York during December 1919 and January
1920. Since that time the existence of the book seems to have
been forgotten, and it was entirely overlooked by Mr. C. H.
Collins Baker when making his *Catalogue of Blake's Drawings
and Paintings in the Huntington Library*, issued in 1938. Photostats of the whole book were recently supplied at my request by

the Librarian of the Huntington Library, by whose courtesy I am enabled to make the present description.

Robert Blake's beginnings as an artist in 1777 did not give any great promise of future eminence. His association with his brother has, however, led to his being remembered as an original draughtsman of considerable power. Some of his drawings were kept by William and passed after his death in 1827 into the possession of Frederick Tatham. Several of these were seen by Gilchrist, who described them as "naif and archaic-looking; rude and faltering, often puerile or absurd in drawing; but are characterised by Blake-like feeling and intention, having in short a strong family likeness to his brother's work. The subjects are from Homer and the Poets." [1] Gilchrist describes particularly Robert's best-known drawing, now in the British Museum Print Room, of a group of people awestruck by an approaching cataclysm. This design was immortalized by William Blake, who used it for what is possibly his earliest experiment in relief-etching on copper, thereby improving Robert's design into a superb work of art. Another sepia wash and pen drawing now in the collection of Mr. W. Graham Robertson shows a huddled group of people cowering before an ancient man who threatens them with upraised arm. I have recently acquired a third drawing, undoubtedly from Robert's hand, though it had been supposed by its former owner, the late H. Buxton Forman, to be by William himself. It represents a Druid grove with two groups of male and female figures in long robes standing between two rows of trees, the branches forming a green roof over their heads (Plate 5). The figures are painted with bright water-colour washes and the composition somehow has distinction, though it is not well drawn if judged by any ordinary standards. Robert

[1] Gilchrist, *loc. cit.* p. 50.

Blake's archaic manner is, in fact, individual and original, and it is the more remarkable that his most distinguished composition, "The King and Queen of the Fairies" (Plate 3), has until recently been unrecognized, and has indeed been passed by many authorities, including Gilchrist, as the work of his brother. By far the most valuable manuscript of William Blake that has come down to us intact is the note-book sometimes known as *The Rossetti MS*. This book is fully described in the next chapter. It is enough to say now that it was clearly treasured by William primarily because it had belonged to Robert, who made sketches and drawings on some of the leaves at the beginning. Several of these are very slight drawings in pencil, but two are compositions in water-colour. The first of these, on page 9, represents a knight in armour rushing from beneath a Gothic cloister. On the right a woman in a long dress is flying away from him through a forest of slender tree trunks (Plate 4). This has been thought to be an illustration of a "Gothic" novel, but its subject has not been identified. The second drawing is of two crowned fairies reclining in a rose-like flower. Over them hang two other bell-shaped flowers with a circle of little figures dancing beneath one of them. It has been called "The King and Queen of the Fairies", and, on the assumption that it was by William, was adapted by Frederick Shields for the cover design of the second edition of Gilchrist's *Life of Blake* published in 1880. It was also used in an altered form by William himself in plate 5 of *The Song of Los*, 1795, one of his illuminated books. In this the King and Queen are lying on two lilies under a dark starry sky. In all these drawings in the Notebook the stiff and angular lines of the figures are unmistakably those of Robert Blake, their style being quite different from that of William, as can be seen by comparing them with any of the other drawings in the book. "The King and

WILLIAM AND ROBERT

Queen of the Fairies" is a composition of imagination and great beauty, and suggests that Robert Blake at the time of his death was shewing, under William's influence, signs of developing into an artist of considerable power, even though he was still deficient in the niceties of accurate drawing, which were not fostered by a drawing master who himself did not believe in "copying nature". This design by itself is convincing evidence of the aesthetic feeling which bound Robert and William in a strange community of spirit both during their lives and after Robert's early death.

II

BLAKE'S NOTEBOOK

STUDENTS OF THE LIFE and works of William Blake have long been aware of the existence of a manuscript volume containing a varied collection of his writings, interspersed with drawings and sketches. The book has been called at different times *The MS. Book*, *The Rossetti MS.*, or *Ideas of Good and Evil*, but its nature is best indicated by the title assigned to it here, *Blake's Notebook*. All serious students of Blake have realized the extraordinary richness of its contents, but few have been privileged to handle it themselves, and so to obtain at first-hand the full flavour of its associations. It is at once evident that Blake himself placed a high value on his *Notebook*, for it cannot have been economy alone that induced him to keep this apparently insignificant volume beside him for forty years, turning to it again and again to confide to its pages the most intimate outpourings of his genius, until it was filled from end to end. The book was turned this way and that in order that every corner might be used, and ultimately extra leaves had to be inserted to accommodate the later portions of the last poem which Blake tried to cram into it. During the last seven years of his life he added nothing more because the book was full, but it was preserved among his papers, and by a fortunate chance fell, twenty years after his death, into the hands of Dante Gabriel Rossetti. From that day, the 30th of April 1847, *Blake's Notebook* has been treated with the reverence it deserves, and has recently been reproduced in facsimile so

that its beauty and its interest may be diffused over a wider
circle.

The book consists of 58 leaves, measuring 19·6 × 15·7 cm.
It has been paginated consecutively 1-116, and is made up of
one gathering of 10 leaves, and four gatherings of 16 and 18
leaves alternately. The paper has no water-mark. A sheet, forming 2 leaves, of different and smaller paper is added at the end.
The manner in which Blake used the book may be reconstructed
from an examination of its contents, though the initial fact of
interest to be noted is that it almost certainly belonged first, not
to William Blake, but to his younger brother, Robert. On pages
5, 7, 9, 11 and 13 are sketches and drawings which have always,
until recently, been assigned with the rest of the contents of the
book to William Blake. But their lines are such that this belief
cannot any longer be held. The figures delineated on these pages
have a stiff and angular character quite different from that of
figures drawn by William Blake, as comparison with any of the
other drawings in the book will shew. They have, on the other
hand, much in common with the amateurish drawing now in the
British Museum which is authenticated as the work of Robert
Blake and with others by him given a few years ago to the Tate
Gallery. This association with Robert Blake had not been noticed
until I drew attention to it in the introduction to the Nonesuch
facsimile of the *Notebook*.

Robert Blake's relation to his brother and the character of his
drawings have already been described. The feeling that existed
between them was evidently very deep, and this provides the
clue to the motive that made William use and treasure the *Notebook* from the day of Robert's death until his own.

When Blake first began to use the book he filled the pages
chiefly with rough sketches for a variety of subjects. These in-

clude ideas for several of the decorations in *Songs of Experience*, *The Marriage of Heaven and Hell*, *Europe* and *America*, and for most of those in *Visions of the Daughters of Albion*. There is also a long series of drawings for "emblems", which, according to the numbers attached to them, Blake arranged and rearranged several times, though he ultimately used only seventeen of them in the small book of engravings known as *The Gates of Paradise*, issued in 1793. The drawings also include two profiles of Blake himself (pp. 66 and 67, Plate 7), a head of his wife (p. 82) and an intimate domestic scene on page 4, which is supposed to represent Blake and his wife together. It is also on this page that the title "Ideas of Good and Evil" has been scrawled; although it remains uncertain to what this should refer, it certainly was not meant as a title for the whole book.

Having used the volume as a sketch-book consecutively from his brother's beginnings until about the year 1793, Blake then turned it round, and began to write poems in it from the other end. This group of poems, including first drafts of several of the *Songs of Experience* (Plate 8), occupies pages 115-98 of the reversed book. It was then laid aside for a time until, during the period of his residence at Felpham, 1800–3, he again used it for a short series of poems and fragments which are written from the beginning of the book on pages 2-14. He picked it up again in 1807 to enter some desultory memoranda, including quotations from Aphra Behn and Dryden which had taken his fancy in reading Bysshe's *Art of Poetry*. Two years later he again began to fill the unused spaces, this time with the scurrilous doggerel on his friends and enemies and with the long prose pieces known as "Public Address", in vindication of his engraving of "The Canterbury Pilgrims", and "A Vision of the Last Judgment", describing his large painting of that subject. These

are written haphazard wherever room could be found, and consist of fragments which are not consecutive but were jotted down
in the heat of the moment as he thought of them. These are all to
be assigned to the years 1808–11, when he was feeling annoyed
and humiliated by his failure to obtain recognition through the
exhibition of his pictures and his "Canterbury Pilgrims". By
this time hardly a corner of the book remained unfilled, and it
was laid aside for some years until, in 1818, Blake again took it
up for the composition of his great philosophical poem, *The
Everlasting Gospel*. This is in unconnected fragments scattered
about in different parts of the book (Plate 6), and ultimately
some of it was written in several separate leaves of paper. One of
these was the last page of a folded leaf from a printed book
carrying the catchword *And*, on the first three pages of which
Blake had written the draft of a prospectus of the "Canterbury
Pilgrims" engraving, presumably composed in 1809. These two
leaves are now bound in at the end of the volume, but the remainder of *The Everlasting Gospel* has long been separated
from it.

  After Blake's death in 1827 the *Notebook* remained in the possession of his wife, by whom it is said to have been given to a
brother of his young friend and disciple, Samuel Palmer. The
next event in its history is recorded by Dante Gabriel Rossetti
on the fly-leaf at the beginning: "I purchased this original M.S.
of Palmer, an attendant in the Antique Gallery at the British
Museum, on the 30th April, 1847. Palmer knew Blake person-
ally, and it was from the artist's wife that he had the present M.S.
which he sold me for 10ˢ. Among the sketches there are one or
two profiles of Blake himself. D.G.C.R." It has usually been
supposed that Rossetti was referring to Samuel Palmer, but this
is clearly impossible, since he was never attached in any capacity

to the staff of the British Museum. His brother William, however, was appointed to the Antique Gallery in 1848,[1] and the reference is clearly to him, though there is no further record of his having been a friend either of Blake or of his wife. The half-sovereign was actually supplied by Rossetti's brother, William, whose pocket was less depleted than his own.

Rossetti contemplated publishing part of the MS., and on November 1, 1860, wrote to William Allingham: "A man (one Gilchrist, who lives next door to Carlyle, and is as near him in other respects as he can manage) wrote to me the other day, saying he was writing a life of Blake, and wanted to see my manuscript by that genius. Was there not some talk of *your* doing something in the way of publishing its contents? I know William [Rossetti] thought of doing so, but fancy it might wait long for his efforts; and I have no time, but really think its contents ought to be edited, especially if a new *Life* gives a 'shove to the concern' (as Spurgeon expressed himself in thanking a liberal subscriber to his Tabernacle). I have not yet engaged myself any way to said Gilchrist on the subject, though I have told him he can see it here if he will give me a day's notice."[2] Rossetti ultimately lent the volume to Gilchrist in 1861, and after Gilchrist's death in that year himself edited a selection from the MS. which was printed in the second volume of Gilchrist's *Life of Blake*, 1863. He had already made a transcript (part of the paper is dated 1844, but the transcript must have been made some years later than this) of most of the poems, which he had bound up with the MS., heading it: "Verse and Prose by William Blake (Natus 1757: obiit 1827). All that is of any value

[1] See Mona Wilson's *Life of Blake* (Nonesuch Press, 1927), p. 35. Presumably Rossetti had met Palmer before he came to be employed at the British Museum.
[2] *Letters of D. G. Rossetti to William Allingham* (London, 1897), p. 237.

in the foregoing pages has been copied out. D.G.C.R." He there introduced a number of alterations, correcting what he considered were imperfections in the metre, and supplying emendations, often quite unnecessary, though he did not in the printed selection adopt all the changes made in the first transcript. He wrote to Gilchrist: "I am glad you approve of my rather unceremonious shaking up of Blake's rhymes. I really believe that is what ought to be done. . . ."

He changed his mind later, however, and in 1874 wrote to his brother that he would not then have made so many changes.[1] The harm, however, was already done; later editors followed Rossetti's text, and so corrupt versions were perpetuated. Further extracts were made by Swinburne for his *Critical Essay*, 1868, especially from *The Everlasting Gospel*, and W. M. Rossetti added to his brother's selections in his Aldine edition of Blake's poems, first published in 1874, though this text is scarcely better than its predecessor of 1863.

After Rossetti's death in 1882 *Blake's Notebook*, or *The Rossetti MS.* as it was henceforth to be known, was sold with his library at an auction held at his house, 16 Cheyne Walk, Chelsea. It was lot 483, offered on the third day, July 7, 1882, and it made £110. Presumably it was then acquired by the bookcollector, F. S. Ellis, with whose collection it was again sold at Sotheby's on November 18, 1885, on this occasion being bought by Ellis and Scrutton for £85. In the following year it was traded across the Atlantic, and came into the hands of the New York dealers, Dodd, Mead and Co. From them it was bought by the late William Augustus White of Brooklyn, who added his signature on the fly-leaf with date "26 January, '87". From this date onwards successive Blake scholars have been

[1] *Letters of D. G. Rossetti to William Allingham* (London, 1897), pp. 264-65.

deeply indebted to W. A. White for his readiness to collaborate in elucidating the manuscript. About 1890 he sent the book to Quaritch in London in order that E. J. Ellis and W. B. Yeats might use it for their three-volume edition of the *Works*, published in 1893. A transcript was made for Ellis, but this again contained many inaccuracies. Ten years later White supplied Dr. John Sampson of Liverpool with material for a very much more accurate text of all the lyrical poems in the manuscript, which were incorporated in the Oxford editions of 1905 and later years. Finally, in 1924 he had the entire manuscript photographed for me, and I was thus enabled to prepare a new and carefully revised text for the Nonesuch edition of Blake's *Writings*, published in 1925. This text gave all the alterations and deletions made by Blake and included almost every word capable of being deciphered.

After the late owner's death, the book passed to his daughter, Mrs. Frances White Emerson of Cambridge, Mass., who brought it again to England and allowed me to keep it for the greater part of a year. I was thus enabled to familiarize myself still further with the text and to satisfy myself that as perfect a text as was humanly possible had been obtained. Some years later Mrs. Emerson put students of Blake still further in her debt by allowing the Nonesuch Press to reproduce the whole MS. in collotype facsimile. This was published in 1935, and was accompanied by a reprint of the text I had prepared in 1925. Unfortunately, this was set up in France by a compositor who did not understand English, and the publisher's urgency deprived me of the opportunity of correcting the proofs myself. The proof-reader, although represented by the publisher as competent and working from an already printed text, nevertheless failed to eliminate some gross typographical errors for which I received the blame—not unnaturally, since my name appeared on the title-page as "editor"! About the same time the late Max Plowman convicted me of making an omission when he borrowed my photographs of the MS. and with great difficulty succeeded in deciphering some very dim pencil marks on page 116. The result of his labours is quoted on page 84 of the present volume. The actual discovery was not, as the reader will learn, one that adds anything to the glory of Blake's name, and the passage may even have been purposely obscured by him, but it does at least testify to the zeal of Blake students and editors in their unflagging quest for every vestige of his recorded mind. The same can be claimed for a not altogether dissimilar discovery of my own, due to my recent acquisition of A. C. Swinburne's transcript of Blake's scatological verses, " When Klopstock England defied". For many years past the last four lines but two of this doggerel have been quite illegible, though it seems they were still decipherable when Swinburne had access to the MS., that is before Rossetti's death in 1882, so that I am now able to provide a complete text—admittedly a contribution of very dubious value.

Rossetti had the manuscript bound in half-calf with his transcript at the end. This binding had become weak, and Mrs. Emerson has recently had the volume rebound in levant morocco with interleaving to protect the pages from further damage by rubbing against one another. Much of the writing had already become very difficult to read, but *Blake's Notebook* is now preserved for posterity, both in its original form and in the Nonesuch facsimile, which gives a faithful representation of Blake's urgent genius. .

POETICAL

SKETCHES.

By W. B.

LONDON:

Printed in the Year M DCC LXXXIII.

III

"POETICAL SKETCHES"

WILLIAM BLAKE's *Poetical Sketches* were first printed in 1783 in a slender octavo of 38 leaves when their author was aged twenty-six. The poems had mostly been written during his boyhood, beginning, according to the unsigned introductory "Advertisement", with his twelfth and extending to his twentieth year. Information as to the circumstances in which the book was printed is given by John Thomas Smith, Keeper of Prints and Drawings in the British Museum, in his account of Blake in *Nollekens and his Times*, 1828. Smith had met Blake about 1784 at the house of the Rev. Henry Mathew in Rathbone Place, where Mrs. Mathew entertained parties of interesting people, including Blake and John Flaxman, and according to Smith it was Mathew and Flaxman who had together defrayed the cost of printing the *Poetical Sketches*. There is good reason for believing in Flaxman's disinterested generosity, for Blake's letters shew that he regarded him for many years with the deepest gratitude and affection, Flaxman having undoubtedly been one of his earliest and closest friends. A rift occurred later, but this is not relevant to the present inquiry.

Blake's childhood and the contemporary influences which helped to shape the poems in *Poetical Sketches* have been critically examined by Miss Ruth Lowery in her very interesting book, *Windows of the Morning* (Yale University Press, 1940), and she is inclined to rate Blake's debt to Flaxman as very high

23

indeed. Partly she bases her conclusions on a document which has recently come to light in an American collection and runs as follows:

Mr. Blake with Compts. sends Mr. Flaxman a Draf$^{t.}$ for £100 and begs to have a Receipt.

Essex Street
9 *Mch.*

The watermark in the paper gives the maker as G. Jones but the date has been cut away. Miss Lowery states that "G. Jones is Griffith Jones, of Hertfordshire, who, between 1804 and 1810, made paper at the Nash Mills, now owned by John Dickinson and Company, Limited. Preserved there are the original moulds upon which G. Jones made paper, and a minute comparison and measurement of the watermark identified 1806 as the date when the sheet of paper was made" (*Windows of the Morning*, p. 50). Miss Lowery therefore concludes that in 1806 Blake was owing Flaxman a considerable sum of money, part of which was probably advanced for the printing of *Poetical Sketches* twenty-three years before. There is, however, more than one good reason for rejecting this conclusion as untenable. In the first place, Miss Lowery has chosen to ignore the fact that the document is not in the handwriting of William Blake, though there is some superficial resemblance to his hand. Secondly, it is known, as Miss Lowery herself states, that a firm of lawyers named Blake did business in Essex Street during most of the years between 1783 and 1828, though there is not the slightest reason for supposing that William Blake was related to, or was even acquainted with, his namesakes. The transaction between Flaxman and the lawyer Blake can, in fact, be identified by reference to a paper by Mr. Edward Croft Murray, F.S.A., on "An Account Book of

John Flaxman".[1] From this it appears that Robert Blake of
14 Essex Street, Strand, acted as intermediary between Flaxman
and a Committee of Wykehamists in the affair of erecting the
monument to Dr. Joseph Warton in Winchester Cathedral. A
payment for £100 is stated to have been made on March 9,
1804, so that evidently the dating of the watermark was only
approximate.

The only financial transaction between William Blake and
Flaxman of which there is complete evidence relates to a payment made to Blake on December 14, 1799, on account of three
copper-plate engravings of a Statue of Britannia. These were in
illustration of Flaxman's *Letter to the Committee for Raising the
Naval Pillar or Monument*, London, 1799, and Blake's receipt
(now in the library of Haverford College, Haverford, Pa.)
shews that he received eight guineas for the engravings, with
12s. 8d. added for the copper. This document is entirely in
Blake's hand, and is signed by him. It is improbable that
Flaxman would have paid Blake this relatively small sum if he
was already creditor since 1783 for a much larger amount.

The cost of composition cannot in any event have been large,
and the number of copies printed was certainly small—fifty
would seem to be a reasonable guess in view of the fact that only
twenty-two copies are known to have survived to the present
time. It may be assumed that the printing was done in London
since all the people concerned lived there, and the eighteenth-
century press-work scales in London are known, so that the
approximate cost of printing fifty copies of the book can be
calculated, given the necessary expert knowledge. This know-

[1] Published in the Walpole Society's vol. xxviii, 1939–40, p. 70. Attention was drawn
to this by Dr. C. F. Bell in a letter to *The Times Literary Supplement*, March 31, 1945.
The Account Book is in the British Museum, Add. MSS. 39, 784. BB.

ledge has been applied by Mr. Ellic Howe and the result is set out below in detail:

POETICAL SKETCHES

	£	s.	d.
9½ sheets of demy, 76 pp. of which 4 blank—			
Approximately 85,000 ens @ 4d. per 1,000	1	10	0
Author's corrections (if any), say 5 hrs.	0	1	8
Make up 76 pp. incl. 2 blanks and set title page			
Lead out verses as required, say 6 pp. per hour	0	4	0
Impose 9 formes @ 8 pp. + 1 @ 4 pp.	0	4	0
Press work @ 6d. per token, 2 men at press, 9 sheets	0	9	0
Warehouse work = fold and stitch, etc.	0	4	0
	£2	12	8
Add 100% for overheads (contemporary practice)	2	12	8
Paper = say 5 sheets of demy per copy: 50 copies = ½ ream	0	10	0
Profit on paper	0	2	0
	£5	17	4

Total cost, say £6 0s. 0d., or nearly 2/5 per copy.

The typography of *Poetical Sketches* suggests that it was entrusted to a small and not particularly competent shop. Lieutenant-Colonel W. E. Moss has noticed that the type and layout of the *Poetical Works* of Scott of Amwell, printed for J. Buckland, 1782, is almost identical with that of *Poetical Sketches*. Furthermore four of the engravings in this book were made by Blake after Stothard, and this might have brought Blake into contact with the printer shortly before his poems were to be set up in type. Again, however, as in *Poetical Sketches*, there is no printer's imprint, and Blake did not work again for the publisher Buckland so that this line of investigation leads us no further.

No part of the original manuscript of the pieces published in *Poetical Sketches* has survived, so that the printed pages are the sole authority for the text. This authority would be good if it could be asserted that Blake himself had certainly seen and corrected proofs of the book, but it seems unlikely that he did so, for he would not have passed a number of typographical errors which annoyed him so much afterwards that he was at some trouble to correct them in the copies given to his friends. The statement in the "Advertisement" that since the time of their composition the author of the poems "has been deprived of the leisure requisite to such a revisal of these sheets, as might have rendered them less unfit to meet the public eye", clearly refers to the poems themselves and not to the printed proof-sheets, since the "Advertisement" was certainly written before the poems were printed, not afterwards. It is possible, as has been suggested, that Blake resented the opening of the second paragraph of the "Advertisement"—"Conscious of the irregularities and defects to be found in almost every page, his friends . . ."; nevertheless he usually allowed copies of the books to reach these friends without removing the offending leaf, and it may be that more has been made of this cause of offence than it really deserves.

Study of other MSS. from Blake's hand shows that his punctuation was apt to be perfunctory or even misleading, and it is evident that the printer of *Poetical Sketches* was sometimes uncertain how to deal with it. This has provided several interesting problems for Blake's editors, notably in three places:

(1) In "To Winter" page 4, lines 6-7, the text reads,

> . . . his storms are unchain'd, sheathed
> In ribbed steel, I dare not lift mine eyes;

Here the sense seems to demand an interchange of comma and semi-colon,

> . . . his storms are unchain'd, sheathed
> In ribbed steel; I dare not lift mine eyes,

(2) In "Fair Elenor", page 8, the text reads,

> As the deer wounded Ellen flew over
> The pathless plain; as the arrows that fly
> By night; destruction flies, and strikes in darkness,
> She fled from fear, till at her house arriv'd.

This clearly demands a full-stop after the "darkness", and in my Nonesuch edition I further emended the punctuation to read,

> . . .; as the arrows that fly
> By night, destruction flies, and strikes in darkness.

Blake commonly, however, used the semi-colon in an unconventional way, and the second emendation is perhaps unnecessary.

(3) In "Blind-Man's Buff", page 28, lines 11-20, the text reads,

> Such are the fortunes of the game,
> And those who play should stop the same
> By wholesome laws; such as all those
> Who on the blinded man impose.
> Stand in his stead as long a-gone
> When men were first a nation grown;
> Lawless they liv'd—till wantonness
> And liberty began t'increase;
> And one man lay in another's way,
> Then laws were made to keep fair play.

Loose construction and careless punctuation have both contributed to ambiguity of meaning. In the Nonesuch text (1925) I tried to give the passage its greatest amount of meaning,

> . . . laws, such as—all those
> Who on the blinded man impose
> Stand in his stead; as, long a-gone
> When men were first a nation grown,

"POETICAL SKETCHES"

Lawless they liv'd—till wantonness
And liberty began t'increase,
And one man lay in another's way;
Then laws were made to keep fair play.

If this amount of interference is distasteful, readers may amend it as they please.

The remaining irregularities in punctuation are less important and need not be discussed. Unimportant also are various archaic or irregular spellings and minor misprints which do not leave the sense in doubt. Of much greater interest are a number of other errors which Blake himself took the trouble to correct in ink. There are twenty-one copies of *Poetical Sketches* known at the present time. Several bear inscriptions showing that they belonged to Thomas Butts, George Cumberland, John Flaxman, Anna Flaxman, William Hayley, John Linnell, William Long, Samuel Palmer, and Charles Tulk. The last has an inscription, "To Charles Tulk Esq.—from William Blake", the only one, so far as I know, with evidence that it was given by Blake himself. Nevertheless some of them do contain one or more corrections in ink which appear to have been made by the author's hand, and these are naturally of the greatest importance in establishing the text. But before these corrections are specified, attention may be directed to lines 15-18 of "An Imitation of Spenser" (p. 24):

Midas the praise hath gain'd of lengthen'd cares,
    For which himself might deem him ne'er the worse
To sit in council with his modern peers,
    And judge of tinkling rhimes, and elegances terse.

One of Blake's most acute editors, Dr. John Sampson, assumed without discussion that *cares* was here a misprint for *ears*. Miss Lowery pointed out that in no copy of the book so far examined had Blake made this correction, and it would be dangerous to assume that Blake really wrote *ears* when he has corrected other apparently more trivial mistakes. I am now able to set all doubts at rest by the discovery that in the Graham Robertson copy (Q in the census), in which there are a number of other corrections undoubtedly in Blake's hand, the *c* of *cares* has been altered by a stroke of the pen to *e*. The correction is inconspicuous, and may have been overlooked in other copies.

In the same category is the reading on the last page of the book in the prose piece entitled "Samson": "Let us detain thee while I make ready a kid, that thou mayest sit and eat, and tell us of thy name and warfare". Here W. M. Rossetti suggested *wayfare* for *warfare*, but so far this has not the support of Blake's correction.

Attention was first attracted to the author's corrections during a discussion in *The Times Literary Supplement* of the first stanza of the celebrated "Mad Song", which is printed in *Poetical Sketches* (p. 15) as follows:

> The wild winds weep,
>   And the night is a-cold;
> Come hither, Sleep,
>   And my griefs unfold:
> But lo! the morning peeps
>   Over the eastern steeps,
> And the rustling beds of dawn
>   The earth do scorn.

In the issue of *The Times Literary Supplement* for October 9, 1919, Professor H. J. C. Grierson (as he then was) published a letter pleading for the common-sense alteration of *beds* in the penultimate line to *birds*, and deprecating purely aesthetic conclusions such as that of Professor Saintsbury (supported by Dr. John Sampson), who maintained in his *History of English Prosody*, 1910 (vol. iii, p. 11) that the "entire imagery of the poem is *atmospheric*, and the phrase '*beds* of dawn' for the clouds whence sun and moon issue is infinitely fine". To this letter I added another in the issue of October 23 pointing out that the alteration of *beds* to *birds* was not first made, as was usually supposed, by D. G. Rossetti in his selection of Blake's poems printed in the second volume of Gilchrist's *Life* (1863 and 1880), but had been made in 1847 by Robert Southey when reprinting the poem in *The Doctor* (vol. vi). Southey had been acquainted with Blake, and expressed great admiration for his poetic talents. Furthermore I was able to draw attention for the first time to the fact that Blake had himself made the correction in the copy of *Poetical Sketches* which had belonged to Thomas Butts. This book was then in the possession of the late T. J. Wise and is now in the Ashley Library among the British Museum collections. I afterwards found the same correction in two other copies, and Miss Lowery added a third—namely, the Graham Robertson copy, now in the possession of Mr. Kerrison Preston. The reading "birds of dawn" may therefore be accepted as fully established. Sir Herbert Grierson has also drawn attention[1] to the fact that Blake may have taken "rustling" from Macpherson's *Ossian*, where it is a recurrent epithet applied to the sound of birds' wings.

Recently Mr. Preston informed me that his copy contains another important correction in the same stanza of the "Mad Song" which has not been noticed before, though I now find it had also been made by Blake in the Butts' copy. This is the alteration of *unfold* in the fourth line to *infold* with obvious advantage to the meaning. The emendation had already been made by some of Blake's editors to *infold* or *enfold*, though without Blake's authority. The page of *Poetical Sketches* showing these corrections by Blake is reproduced here by Mr. Preston's

[1] In a letter to *The Times Literary Supplement*, April 7, 1945.

permission (Plate 9). The true reading of the first stanza of the "Mad Song" is therefore now established as follows:

> The wild winds weep,
>   And the night is a-cold;
> Come hither, Sleep,
>   And my griefs infold:
> But lo! the morning peeps
>   Over the eastern steeps,
> And the rustling birds of dawn
>   The earth do scorn.

In the first (three-volume) Nonesuch edition of Blake's writings I was able to add a second correction made by the author in the third stanza, line 3, of "To Winter" (p. 4), printed in 1783, as,

> He withers all in silence, and *in* his hand
> Unclothes the earth, and freezes up frail life.

Here he has deleted the second *in*, again with clear advantage to sense and metre.

In the fourth printing (1939) of the Nonesuch one-volume edition I added three more corrections made by him in John Linnell's copy of *Poetical Sketches*, these being:

(1) In "An Imitation of Spenser", page 24, stanza 2, line 5, printed as,

> And love of Folly needs none others curse,

altered to "none *other* curse".

(2) In "King Edward the Third", page 44, lines 18-19:

> . . .; while Reason, in her
> Frail bark, . . .

altered to "in *his* Frail bark".

(3) In the same, page 46, penultimate line, printed as,

> Shall flee away, and leave them all forlorn;

altered to "leave *him* all forlorn".

Miss Lowery adds four more corrections. Two are from the

"POETICAL SKETCHES"

Tulk copy of *Poetical Sketches* now in the Huntington Library, California:

(1) In the "Song", "Love and harmony combine", page 12, stanza 4, line 4, printed as,

> There is love: I hear her tongue

altered to "I hear *his* tongue". This change Dr. Sampson had already made in 1905, though without Blake's authority.

(2) In "Fair Elenor", page 7, stanza 2, lines 1-2, printed as,

> . . . and sunk upon the steps
> On the cold stone her pale cheeks . . .

altered to "her pale *cheek*". The second of these is found also in the Graham Robertson copy, which provides two more:

(3) In "Fair Elenor", page 9, stanza 16, line 1, printed as,

> O Elenor, I am thy husband's head,

altered to read,

> O Elenor, *behold* thy husband's head.

This change was also made in Mrs. Flaxman's copy of the book, and in the Butts copy.

(4) In "To the Evening Star", page 5, line 2, printed as,

> Now whilst the sun rests on the mountains, . . .

whilst is altered to *while*.

This completes the sum of the author's corrections so far detected in various copies of *Poetical Sketches*. The changes demonstrate in an interesting way the necessity for examining carefully every extant copy of a work such as this, printed without the author's supervision and distributed privately to his friends. Only in this way can the text be brought to a state corresponding as nearly as possible to the author's intention.

33

"POETICAL SKETCHES"

CENSUS OF COPIES

In my *Bibliography of Blake*, Grolier Club, 1921, I compiled a census of as many copies of *Poetical Sketches* as I could discover, these amounting to fourteen. Miss Lowery added four more in the *Transactions of the Bibliographical Society*, vol. xvii, 1936, p. 354. This list, together with the added copies that increase the number to twenty-two, is now revised and brought up to date.

(A) British Museum (C.59, v.30). Bound in calf, edges trimmed. Possibly one of Samuel Palmer's copies; see copy G below. Acquired for the British Museum in June 1890, from Quaritch for £42. Then unbound.

(B) Butts copy. In original blue-gray wrappers, untrimmed, as issued. Sold at Sotheby's, May 2, 1906 (lot 801, £60). Acquired by the late T. J. Wise, and now in the Ashley Library at the British Museum (Ashley 2366). Contains four corrections in Blake's hand.

(C) Tulk copy. Inscribed "Charles Tulk Esq.—from William Blake". Bound in citron morocco, gilt, by the Club Bindery. Sold in 1906 (B. F. Stevens, £109). Resold with the Hoe Library pt. I, at the Anderson Galleries, New York, April 26, 1911 (lot 389, $275). Now in the H. E. Huntington Library, San Marino, California. Contains corrections in Blake's hand.

(D) George Cumberland copy, with his signature on the title-page. Bound in half-calf, with a print of "The man sweeping the interpreter's parlour" inserted as frontispiece, and with Cumberland's book-plate, engraved by Blake, inside the cover. The frontispiece is inscribed, "The Parable of the relapsed sinner & her 7 Devils", but not in Blake's hand. Given by Cumberland to John Linnell, and sold at Sotheby's with Linnell's books June 3, 1918 (lot 3, Pickering, £60).

Acquired by the late Beverly Chew. Sold at the Chew sale at the Anderson Galleries, New York, December 8, 1924 (lot 28, Rosenbach, $900). Now in the library of Mr. John J. Emery. Exhibited at the Philadelphia Museum of Art, 1939, No. 1.

(E) William Long copy, inscribed on the title-page "To Mr. Long from J. Flaxman". Now bound in green morocco by Macdonald. It was offered to me by Mr. T. Thorp of Guildford for £60 in December 1919, and was then bound in half-calf with several dramatic works. Afterwards acquired by Col. Hughes, Philadelphia, and sold with his books by the American Art Association, April 24, 1924 (lot 58, $525). Acquired by George C. Smith, jr., and sold with his library at the Parke-Bernet Galleries, New York, November 2, 1938 (lot 9, Gabriel Wells, $350). Present owner not traced. Contains corrections in Blake's hand. (William Long, 1747–1818, was a surgeon, and a friend both of Flaxman and Hayley; see copy S.)

(F) Mrs. Anna Flaxman copy, with three additional songs inscribed, but not in Blake's hand, on the flyleaves. These are, "Song 1st by a Shepherd", "Song 2nd by a Young Shepherd", "Song 3rd by an Old Shepherd". The second of these is a variant version of "Laughing Song" from *Songs of Innocence*. The first and third were first printed by R. H. Shepherd in B. M. Pickering's edition of *Songs of Innocence and of Experience*, 1868. This copy of *Poetical Sketches* is bound in contemporary red morocco, yellow edges, and has at the top of the title-page the inscription "present (*del.*) from Mrs. Flaxman May 15 1784"; the recipient is not indicated. Other inscriptions on the flyleaves are, "Reed's Sale 1807", and "ex Bibliotheca Heberiana, fourth portion, sold by Evans, 9 Dec., 1834". There is a book-plate inscribed "J.H.A. 1834", perhaps that of J. H. Anderdon. Later history unknown until it was sold at Sotheby's from an anonymous source, March 22, 1918 (lot 448, Edwards, £52). It was lent to me by Mr. Francis Edwards, and I published a full description in *Notes and Queries*, September 24, 1910. Now in the Alexander Turnbull Library, Wellington, New Zealand. There are numerous corrections in the text and in the margins in both pen and pencil. Most of these are

D

the same as were made by Blake in other copies, but some seem to be suggestions made by friends, perhaps the Flaxmans.

(G) Samuel Palmer copy, containing a pencil note by John Linnell stating that it was one of three copies found by him at Palmer's house. It was then unbound. Now bound in half-morocco, trimmed. Sold at Hodgson's in 1906 (Maggs, £16 : 5s.). Afterwards acquired by Prof. G. H. Palmer, and now in the Library of Wellesley College. (The other two copies found in sheets in March 1890 are H and N below.)

(H) John Pearson copy, bound in green morocco, gilt, by F. Bedford, untrimmed. Sold at Sotheby's November 7, 1916 (lot 40, Dobell, £51). Acquired by Herschel V. Jones, and sold with his library at the Anderson Galleries, New York, December 2, 1918 (lot 121, G. D. Smith, $445). In 1936 in the library of Mr. Carl H. Pforzheimer, New York.

(I) T. G. Arthur copy, bound in red morocco, gilt, by Lortic frères, untrimmed. Title-page and Advertisement leaf repaired. Sold at Sotheby's July 15, 1914 (lot 46, G. D. Smith, £56). Sold by G. D. Smith on November 8, 1918, to A. E. Newton for $400. Sold with the Newton Library at the Parke-Bernet Galleries, New York, on April 16, 1941 (lot 124, Papantonio, $225). Present owner not traced. Exhibited at the Philadelphia Museum of Art, 1939, No. 2.

(K) R. A. Potts copy, bound in calf, gilt, by F. Bedford. Pp. 49-70 in facsimile. Sold at Sotheby's, February 20, 1913 (lot 71, £8 : 5s.). Sold again at Sotheby's, July 22, 1918 (Protheroe, £10); at Sotheby's December 17, 1919 (G. D. Smith, £8); at the Anderson Galleries, New York, April 28, 1921 ($10). In 1936 said to be in the possession of Mr. Francis J. Underhill. Offered for sale in London by Raphael King, cat. 34, January 1940, for £65. Now in the U.S.A.

(L) A copy sold at Sotheby's, "The Property of a Lady", on May 2, 1911 (lot 321, Quaritch, £49). Stated to be bound in contemporary red straight-grained morocco, gilt, gilt edges. Acquired by H. T. Butler, and sold with his library at Hodgson's, June 14, 1934 (lot 439, Robinson, £92). Acquired by Lord Rothschild, and still in his library.

The present owner informed Miss Lowery that he is suspicious of the binding, because the end-papers do not appear to be original. An inscription on the title-page has become illegible owing to washing.

(M) H. Buxton Forman copy, bound in blue morocco, gilt, by Roger de Coverly, with a sonnet by Buxton Forman in his hand on the fly-leaf and corrections in the text copied by him from copy B. Sold at the Anderson Galleries, New York, March 15, 1920 (pt. 1, lot 35, $410). Present owner not traced.

(N) Thomas Gaisford copy, bound in green morocco, gilt, by F. Bedford, untrimmed. Sold with the Gaisford Library at Sotheby's, April 23, 1890 (lot 184, Quaritch, £48). Acquired by B. B. Macgeorge. Sold with the Macgeorge Library at Sotheby's, July 9, 1924 (lot 109, Quaritch, £118). Offered by Quaritch, November, 1924, for £135. Acquired by Willis Vickery, and sold with his library at the Anderson Galleries, New York, March 3, 1933 (Beyer, $975). Now in the collection of Mr. Chauncey B. Tinker, Yale University.

(O) W. E. Moss copy, bound in red morocco, gilt, by Fazakerley. Sold with the Moss collection at Sotheby's, March 2, 1937 (lot 141, Sawyer, £80). Now in U.S.A. Owner not traced.

(P) Stirling copy, bound in green morocco, gilt, by Rivière, untrimmed. Pp. 57-70 in facsimile. Acquired by General Archibald Stirling of Keir from Quaritch, about 1900, and now in the possession of Lt.-Col. William Stirling.

(Q) Graham Robertson copy, bound in green morocco, gilt, by Zaehnsdorf, gilt edges. Title-page mended, and Advertisement leaf in facsimile. First recorded as sold with the library of Maurice Johnson, Sotheby's, March 21, 1898 (C. Brown, £6 : 17 : 6). Sold again at Hodgson's, Nov. 20, 1901 (Quaritch, £12 : 10s.). Bought from Quaritch by Mr. W. Graham Robertson, and recently given by him to Mr. Kerrison Preston. Contains corrections in Blake's hand.

(R) W. A. White copy, unbound, untrimmed, and unopened. Now in the possession of Dr. A. S. W. Rosenbach, New York. Exhibited at the Philadelphia Museum of Art, 1939, No. 3.

"POETICAL SKETCHES"

(S) William Hayley copy, bound, edges trimmed. A faded and cropped inscription on the title-page has been read as, "To William Haley from J. Flax[man]". It was presumably this copy that was mentioned by Flaxman in a letter to Hayley, April 26 (1783), "I have left a pamphlet of poems with Mr. Long, which he will transmit to Eartham; they are the writings of a Mr. Blake you have heard me mention: his education will plead sufficient excuse to your liberal mind for the defects of his work" (*Letters of W. B.*, ed. Russell, 1906, p. 51). The book was in the Kemble-Devonshire collection of drama, formed about 1825, and is now in the H. E. Huntington Library, California. The information about the inscription was given to Miss Lowery by the Assistant Curator of Rare Books in 1934.

(T) John Linnell copy, bound in half-calf together with copy K of *A Descriptive Catalogue*. Inscribed, "John Linnell 38 Porchester Terrace Bayswater 1846", and "To James T[homas] L[innell] 1866". From Linnell's son, James, it passed to his grandson Herbert, and finally was sold in 1937 by his great-grandson, John Linnell, to Lessing J. Rosenwald, Philadelphia. It is now in the Lessing J. Rosenwald Collection, Library of Congress. This copy contains five corrections in Blake's hand, as recorded above.

(U) Hornby Library copy, bound in calf, gilt, by F. Bedford. Pp. 49-70 in facsimile. Similar to copy K above, and the sale there recorded at Sotheby's, July 22, 1918, may have been of this copy. Now in the H. F. Hornby Library, City of Liverpool Public Libraries.

(V) Locker-Lampson copy, in blue-grey wrappers, untrimmed, in green morocco case. Sold at the Parke-Bernet Galleries, New York, January 9, 1945 (lot 70). Now in the library of Dr. James B. Clements.

(W) University College, London. Not available for description.

There are a few other sale records of unidentifiable copies not included here. Alexander Gilchrist stated in the *Life* (1863) that he had found the book so rare that he had had to use a

"POETICAL SKETCHES"

borrowed copy. Miss Lowery notes that Sotheby's catalogue for July 16-20, 1886, lists an uncut copy said to have been formerly Gilchrist's property. As Gilchrist died in 1863, the catalogue statement is presumably inaccurate. Perhaps it was the borrowed copy which had remained among his books.

J. Warner Gent. to 1570, with give vouching
Administrator Apríl. as 100. paid by his father

Joseph Perking Son of Theo. of Thomasgate in the
C.y Rent Gent to Theo. Smith of Sweetings Alley
R. of J. £28. 100. paid by his father.

Wm Blake Son of James of Boog Street Kenby
Gray
Bound to James Boove of Lincolne Inn
fields J.y. as £52. 10 paid by his father

John Harris Son of Rich. of Clerkenwell Close
Coopr to James Simmons J.P. John Square
Clerkenwell Printer J. R. of No Money.

Thos. lately Wood of No. of the Parish of
Stepham in the C.y of York Weaver to Jno.
Seer of Shoreditch good beater J.y. of Jno. £5
in Charity by his thumb Wood sure of Whitechapel

IV

THE ENGRAVER'S APPRENTICE

THE STORY OF BLAKE's apprenticeship to James Basire, engraver, of Great Queen Street, Lincoln's Inn Fields, has been told by Gilchrist, but it has been hitherto incomplete in one important particular, namely the date at which the apprenticeship began. According to Gilchrist, Blake was aged fourteen when he left the drawing-school of Henry Pars to become engraver's apprentice, that is to say, Gilchrist infers, in 1771. Recently, however, Mr. Ellic Howe, while engaged on researches in the records of the Stationers' Company, stumbled on the actual entry of Blake's bond in the Apprentice Register, at Stationers' Hall, and has kindly communicated his discovery to me. The entry (reproduced here by permission of the Worshipful Master of the Company) runs as follows, under the date August 4, 1772:

Wᵐ Blake Son of James of Broad Street Carnaby Market Hosier to James Basire of Great Queen Street Lincoln's Inn fields 7 yʳˢ. £52-10 paid by his Father.

Blake was born on November 28, 1757, and was therefore nearer fifteen than fourteen when he commenced engraver, so that his preliminary training as a draughtsman with Henry Pars lasted somewhat longer than has been supposed.

Gilchrist's chief source of information concerning Blake's early years was the introduction to Benjamin Heath Malkin's *A Father's Memoirs of his Child*, 1806, but the recorded facts are few and Gilchrist's account of the apprentice is necessarily somewhat fanciful. Malkin, however, has provided interesting information concerning Blake's quarrels with his fellow-apprentices, and how he was sent out to make drawings of the tombs in Westminster Abbey and elsewhere. Blake was thus brought early into contact with some of the great figures of English history through their effigies, and several of the engraved heads in Gough's *Sepulchral Monuments in Great Britain* (published in 1786) can be attributed with certainty to his hand. One of those, the "Portrait of Queen Philippa from her Monument", was later vouched for by Stothard who, according to Malkin, "often used to mention this drawing as Blake's, and with praise". Other heads engraved in the same style are those of Henry III, Queen Eleanor, Edward III (Plate 13), Richard II and Anne, his Queen.

All the engravings executed by the apprentices were, of course, signed with Basire's name, so that the work of the juvenile engraver cannot as a rule be identified with certainty. Blake, as Gilchrist points out, is likely to have been employed on plates executed in Basire's shop during those years, for books such as *Archeologia* and *Memoirs of Hollis*, and a careful search of these and other volumes of the period might reveal some interesting sources from which Blake afterwards culled ideas for his own designs. Sometimes a plate can be attributed with confidence to Blake's pencil as well as his graver, and an example of this was recently illustrated by Mr. Ruthven Todd in his *Tracks in the Snow*, 1946. The print appeared as a tail-piece to vol. iii of Jacob Bryant's *New System, or An Analysis, of Ancient Mythology*, 1774–76. It shows a dove bringing a sprig to the Ark, shaped like a crescent moon and floating on the waters under a semicircle of rainbow. Volumes i and ii of the *New System* also

42

have engraved tail-pieces, and those from vols. i and iii are re-produced here. The later one was, as already said, certainly designed by Blake. The earlier one was not so certainly, though probably, also from his hand. Even if drawn by another, the design of intertwined serpents would have appealed to the fancy of a boy who in later years was to use so constantly the symbol of the serpent in his own designs (plate 11).

A characteristic of Blake's mind, the continuity of his ideas over a long period of years, is illustrated in a later chapter by the history of the Job theme. Mr. Ruthven Todd in his book illustrates it again when he draws attention to the fact that the crescentic Ark of his boyhood's design remained in the mind's eye of the artist until he incorporated it in his symbolic system and used it twice in *Jerusalem*, plates 24 and 44, some forty years later. A further search through the numerous plates in vol. ii of the *New System* reveals several other possible sources of ideas which came to fruition during Blake's maturity. Several writers, including the late Laurence Binyon, have commented on the strangely impressive use made by Blake in *Jerusalem* of the man-headed bulls some years before the granite bulls of Nineveh, now in the British Museum, had been discovered by Layard's excavations. It seemed to Binyon to be almost second sight on Blake's part, who could never have rested his bodily eye on anything of the kind. But on plate 16 of the *New System* we find a series of illustrations of this very idea derived from Greek sources (Plate 10). It would not be difficult for the imagination of the mature artist to develop this figure, first absorbed by the boy's mind, into the terrific images of *Jerusalem*.[1]

---

[1] On plate 33 of *Jerusalem* the man-headed animals drawing the plough are more like lions than bulls. It is on plate 46 that the creatures, harnessed by serpents to the Chariot of Time, assume a more bull-like form.

Another symbol encountered several times in the Prophetic Books (*The Four Zoas, Milton* and *Jerusalem*) is the Mundane Egg, signifying the Universe as perceived by the senses. On plate 4 of the *New System* this is illustrated in the most literal fashion, one of the eggs being entwined by a serpent—*Ophis et Ovum Mundanum,*—again an image likely to appeal to Blake. Bryant states (*New System,* vol. i, p. 480) that according to orphic theology the Mundane Egg was produced by Hercules, who was sometimes symbolized by a serpent. Both these figures were taken by Bryant from Vaillant's *Coins of the Colonies* (vol. ii, pp. 331, 136).

Lastly, and most remarkable of all, on plate 2 is illustrated "Zor-Aster Archimagus before an altar with a particular covering like a Cupselis or hive: taken from Kaempfer's Amoenitates Exoticae" (Plate 12). Beneath is a frieze of figures with arms upraised and crossed, a theme which was to appear in 1795 in one of the designs for Young's *Night Thoughts,* in 1809 in the third illustration to Milton's "Hymn on the Nativity",[1] in the water-colour drawing of "David delivered out of Many Waters" from the Butts collection and finally in the supreme design of "When the Morning Stars sang together" designed about 1820 and engraved as plate 14 in *Illustrations of the Book of Job.*[2]

These plates from the *New System* are reproduced here not as works of art, nor even as having been necessarily engraved by Blake during his apprenticeship. They are given as evidence of images which Blake certainly *saw* during his boyhood, and afterwards reproduced and transformed for his own pur-

[1] Reproduced in *Milton's Hymn,* edited by the present writer for the Cambridge University Press, 1923.

[2] On plate 75 of *Jerusalem* is a frieze of angels, perhaps also derived from this source; but the figures have wings alternately raised and lowered, so that they do not intersect like the arms in the other designs.

poses by passing them through the furnace of his creative imagination.

A minor detail of the Ark tail-piece, the palm leaves with which the lower part of the design is framed, Blake used again a few years later in one of his earliest signed engravings, the frontispiece to Commins's *Elegy set to Music*, 1786 (Plate 15). This, his first original book illustration, shows a young sailor springing eagerly from his boat to meet his wife and child, the sentiment and characterization of the figures being strongly reminiscent of Stothard's work. Stothard had not begun making book illustrations, many of which Blake engraved, until 1779, the year in which Blake's time with Basire ended, so that his influence can scarcely have been felt by the apprentice. But in 1784 Blake set up with his fellow apprentice, Parker, as print sellers and dealers, and they even published in that year a pair of prints after designs by Stothard, whose early friendship with Blake and his brother Robert has already been described.

Another glimpse of Blake, the apprentice, may be gained from a glance at his first independent print; the first, that is, that can be identified. Students of his work have long been familiar with the print of "Joseph of Arimathea among the Rocks of Albion". This is signed as "Engraved by W. Blake 1773 from an old Italian Drawing, Michael Angelo pinxit". We now know that in 1773 Blake had been apprenticed only a few months to Basire, and, even had the time been somewhat longer, it seemed incredible that so mature a work as this fine and impressive print could have been produced by a boy of barely sixteen years. The puzzle has been resolved by my discovery a few years ago of a unique and previously unknown print of the first state of this plate. Blake must have kept a pull from the plate in his portfolio, and many years later he wrote at the bottom, "Engraved when I was a beginner at Basire's from a drawing by Salviati after Michael Angelo" (Plate 14). The drawing by Salviati (*i.e.* Gioseffo Porta, 1535–85) has not been identified, but the source of the figure is Michelangelo's fresco of the Crucifixion of St. Peter in the Cappella Paolina at the Vatican. The apprentice's rendering of it, with a background of sea and rocks supplied from his imagination, is undistinguished, though remarkable for a beginner. Although the style is somewhat tame, it is nevertheless not so monotonous and pedestrian as the plates done for his master's eye and to please his customers. It was twenty years later, or more, that Blake again took up his juvenile plate, rubbed the surface down and almost completely re-engraved it, adding strength to the figure and dramatic intensity to the background so that the print was transformed into the mature and characteristic work of art which had seemed so curiously precocious. The boy had chosen the subject because it was from a picture by his idol, Michelangelo, but in the intervening years the young man had been reading Jacob Bryant and the Druidical mythologists, and so he was able to fit the figure into the beginnings of his own mythology, and add the information that "This is One of the Gothic Artists who Built the Cathedrals in what we call the Dark Ages Wandering about in sheep skins & goat skins of whom the World was not worthy; such were the Christians in all Ages". It is interesting to notice that Michelangelo's figure is represented with "the classical foot", that is, with feet having second toes considerably longer than the great toes. This peculiarity was seized upon by the apprentice, who always afterwards drew feet shewing these proportions. The idiosyncrasy was certainly deliberate, for Blake usually drew human hands and feet with particular care, and he directed attention to them when he wrote much later in his life in the description of his picture of the Last Judgment: "I intreat, then, that the Spectator will attend to the Hands & Feet, to the Lineaments of the Countenances; they are all descriptive of Character, & not a line is drawn without intention, & that most discriminate & particular".[1]

Blake's reading during his years of training was certainly extensive among the poets from Spenser to Chatterton, as may be

inferred from his own compositions printed as *Poetical Sketches* in 1783. His enthusiasms in art and artists he has also expressed clearly enough in his *Descriptive Catalogue* and other writings. There is, however, little or no evidence as to what he may have read in art criticism, except for one interesting relic which has been for many years in my own library. This is a copy of Fuseli's translation of the Abbé Winkelmann's *Reflections on the Painting and Sculpture of the Greeks*, London, 1765. On the fly-leaf Blake has written his name, now his earliest surviving signature, and his professional address as engraver's apprentice. The abbreviated form "Lincoln's Inn" for "Great Queen Street, Lincoln's Inn Fields" might arouse suspicions that it was really

[1] *Poetry and Prose* (ed. Keynes, 1939), p. 645.

47

one of his legal namesakes (see p. 24) who had been reading
Fuseli's Winkelmann, were it not that the signature resembles
the artist's later signatures much more closely than those of the
other Blake of which I have seen many examples.

This book seeks to analyse the ideas of Art and Beauty current
among the Greeks, particularly in relation to their exaltation of
the naked human form above all other kinds of beauty. Among
their followers the author admires Blake's idols, Michelangelo
and Raphael, beyond most other artists. There are innumerable
passages in this book which may have sown in Blake's mind
seeds of some of the ideas that afterwards grew to the size, sometimes, of obsessions. Blake's dogma, "Art can never exist without
Naked Beauty displayed",[1] finds its justification in many of
Winkelmann's pages; also his distaste for drawing from models,
his preference for general forms of beauty and ideal images, and
his use of garments which emphasize rather than obscure the
human form.[2] It is true that in his latest years Blake came to
condemn Greek art, because "Grecian is Mathematic Form",
whereas "Gothic is Living Form". This was the result of lump-
ing Greece and Rome together as "Warlike States", which
"never can produce Art".[3] Yet in the *Descriptive Catalogue* of
1809 he had written:

Painting and Sculpture as it exists in the remains of Antiquity and
in the works of more modern genius, is Inspiration, and cannot be
surpassed; it is perfect and eternal. Milton, Shakespeare, Michael
Angelo, Rafael, the finest specimens of Ancient Sculpture and Painting
and Architecture, Gothic, Grecian, Hindoo and Egyptian, are the
extent of the human mind. The human mind cannot go beyond the
gift of God, the Holy Ghost.

[1] The Laocoön plate, *Poetry and Prose* (1939), p. 581.
[2] Coleridge also noticed this peculiarity in his letter to Tulk. See p. 96.
[3] On Virgil, *Poetry and Prose* (1939), p. 583.

So it is probable that the youthful Blake owed much to Greek inspiration under the guidance of Winkelmann and Fuseli, and that this was not counteracted by Jacob Bryant's "low opinion of the Greeks",[1] whose ponderous text had perhaps made less impression on the boy's mind than the copper-plates upon which he was employed.

To conclude these observations on Blake's apprenticeship it may be remarked that James Basire's good training, with his own application to the work, placed him in the first rank among the journeyman engravers of his time. Examination of his plates shews that he could vary his technique at will and equal the best exponents of any of the different methods then in fashion. Blake, the rebel and creator, could always give way to the successor of Blake, the faithful apprentice, when economic necessity pressed its claims.

[1] See Todd's *Tracks in the Snow* (1946), pp. 31-3.

V

ENGRAVERS CALLED BLAKE

THE STUDY of William Blake's output as an engraver of
supreme originality and imagination leads inevitably to a
consideration of his work as a journeyman engraver, which from
the end of his apprenticeship to Basire in 1779 formed an important part of the sources of his very modest livelihood. Many
of these engravings, made as book illustrations after draughts-
men such as Stothard, Flaxman and Fuseli, or done for the
publishers of decorative prints, have little or no importance in
the history of art except in so far as it was Blake's hand that
made them. Yet the more conventional side of his profession was
not without influence on his creative work and possesses also its
biographical interest. Students of Blake have therefore been at
pains to detect and list all the engravings that could be attributed
to him, and indeed many unsigned prints which could not possibly be his have also been fathered on him, sometimes in order
to give a spurious interest and value to goods of no intrinsic merit
whatever. Mrs. Trimmer's series of miserable prints in illustration of the Bible are examples of this tendency. Another source
of confusion has lain in the possibility that there may have been
another, or more than one other, engraver of the same name
working in London at the same time. It was noted by A. G. B.
Russell in 1912 in his *Engravings of William Blake* that there
were three plates in existence bearing the lettering: *Blake sc.
'Change Alley*. One is the frontispiece of a thin volume entitled:

"The Poetry of Various Glees, Songs, &c. as performed at the Harmonists. London: Printed at the Philanthropic Reform, London-Road, St. George's Fields, 1798". The second is a ticket of admission to a concert held on May 28, 1800, in aid of the funds for erecting a naval monument at Greenwich after a design by Flaxman. (William Blake did in fact execute three very trivial engravings for a pamphlet in favour of the same project, a statue of Britannia Triumphant 230 feet high on Greenwich Hill, but this is only a coincidence.) The third is a ticket of admission to the opening of the West Middlesex Water Works on December 4, 1809. Russell accepted these as the work of William Blake, and suggested that 'Change Alley was the address of the printer with whom he worked on these occasions. The Harmonists volume is in my collection. The other two prints are in the British Museum. In my *Bibliography of Blake*, 1921, I was able to add the information that "Blake, Mr., Engraver, No. 6 Exchange-alley, Cornhill—4 copies" appeared in the list of subscribers to Bell's *Shakespeare*, an elaborately illustrated work in twenty volumes, published 1786-88. This seemed to point strongly to the fact that Blake of Exchange-alley was not the same as William Blake the artist and poet, who could have had no possible use for four copies of Bell's *Shakespeare* in 1788. Confirmation of this was provided by Miss Mona Wilson who noted that the London directory for 1795 recorded "W. S. Blake, Engraver" at 16 Exchange Alley (*Life of W. B.*, 1927, p. 318). An undated print of the period showing "A View of Sydney Harbour", now in the British Museum, is signed W. S. Blake, without any address. No. 6 Exchange Alley in the Bell's *Shakespeare* subscription list is probably a misprint for No. 16. Nevertheless the compilers of the catalogue of the very important Blake exhibition held at Philadelphia in 1939 again listed another copy of the Harmonists volume among the works of William Blake, and added two more items of the same kind. One was a card of introduction to the Harmonic Society, undated, but presumably about 1798, with the same lettering as before. The other was the card of L. Parroissien, who taught "Latin, French & English grammatically, with Writing & Accompts", at the Academy, Great Ilford, Essex. This was again undated, but was lettered *Blake Sculpt. Abchurch Lane*, thus introducing a new address, though it may be noted that Exchange Alley and Abchurch Lane are very near one another, both running into Lombard Street on opposite sides.

Further evidence of a conclusive kind can now be added. Lt.-Col. W. E. Moss has recently informed me that he has discovered two more specimens of the work of the " 'Change Alley" Blake. Both are masonic certificates printed on vellum. One is a general form which could be used by any lodge by filling in its name and number. This specimen happened to have been used by the Secretary of the Lodge of Loyalty in Guernsey in 1818, but the engraving was probably made much earlier. It is lettered *Bro Blake sculp. 'Change Alley*. The other certificate was specially engraved for the Lodge of Harmony No. 612 in the Island of Guernsey between the dates 1809 and 1814, when the Lodge was given another number. It is lettered *Bro R. W. Isemonger delint. Bro Blake sculp.* Lastly, I have a note of another trade card lettered: *I. Rowe | Engraver and Printer | 10 Change Alley | Apprentice & Successor to the late Mr. Blake.*

Reference has already been made (see p. 41) to Mr. Ellic Howe's discovery of Blake's being bound apprentice to James Basire in 1772. Another entry in the same Apprentice Register had previously caught his eye a page or two earlier, since it was twice signed "Wm. Blake". From this it appears that on February 5, 1771, Thomas Powell, apprentice of John Bannister, was "Turned by Consent of proper Parties to Wm. Blake of Butcher Hall Lane Newgate Street, Engraver, Citizen, & Clothworker." This entry was signed by all three parties to the transaction, and Wm. Blake signed in addition the statement: "I Promise to make the said apprentice free of the Sta^rs. Co. at the End of his Term". Either, therefore, there was yet another master-engraver called William Blake working in the City at about the same period as the subject of this book was serving his apprenticeship, or it may be that W. S. Blake was already established in business at Butcher Hall Lane as early as 1771.

However this may be, it is now possible to state definitely that a journeyman engraver named W. S. Blake was working from about 1780 to 1810 in the neighbourhood of Lombard Street, first in Abchurch Lane, then at No. 16, and later at No. 10, Exchange Alley. He was a Mason, and was succeeded after his death by his apprentice I. Rowe, and so may now be allowed a separate identity from his more distinguished namesake. His work is of honest insignificance, a quality which, it must be confessed, often characterizes the genuine labours of William Blake, when he was engaged in earning his bread and butter. Finally, it is quite possible that William Blake and W. S. Blake were acquainted with one another, the connecting link being the amateur engraver and print collector, George Cumberland. Already in 1784 Cumberland was thinking, and no doubt talking, about a method of writing poems on copper, an account of which ne communicated to Henry Maty's *New Review*[1]; this is printed n vol. vi, 1784, p. 318, and Cumberland there stated that "the nventor in January last, wrote a poem on copper by means of

---

[1] First noticed by Miss Mona Wilson, *Life of Blake* (1927), p. 23.

this art; and some impressions of it were printed by Mr. Blake, in Exchange-alley, Cornhill, which answered perfectly well, although it had cost very little more time than common writing. Any number of impressions, in proportion to the strength of biting-in may be taken off." A letter [1] written by George Cumberland to his brother Richard in the same year describes the same process, though it is evident that he proposed only to etch his poem on copper without attempting to reverse the writing, so that the print would have to be read with the aid of a mirror.

In his prose burlesque known as *An Island in the Moon*, written about 1787, Blake appears to have been satirizing various contemporary figures, and he makes an unmistakable reference to Cumberland's method of printing as follows:

. . . thus illuminating the manuscript.
"Ay," said she, "that would be excellent."
"Then," said he, "I would have all the wording engraved instead of printed, and at every other leaf a high-finished print—all in three volumes folio,—and sell them for a hundred pounds apiece. They would print off two thousand." [2]

The number, two thousand, was the same as George Cumberland had mentioned in his letter to his brother.

By December 1795 Blake and Cumberland were corresponding as friends, and they may well have been acquainted for some years before this. Blake, however, makes no mention in his writings of the namesake who had printed Cumberland's plates in 1784, though he refers to several of the better-known engravers of his time. Mr. Ruthven Todd has drawn attention [3] to

[1] *The Cumberland Letters* (ed. Black, London, 1912), p. 317.
[2] *Blake's Poetry and Prose* (ed. Keynes, London, 1939), p. 690. The MS. is defective just before this passage.
[3] *The Times Literary Supplement*, February 10, 1945.

the fact that the names of "William Blake" and "W. S. Blake (Writing Engraver)" both appeared in 1797 on a list of signatories to a testimonial to one Alexander Tilloch, who claimed to have devised a method of engraving which would prevent the forging of bank-notes; but even this does not necessarily mean that the two Blakes had met. Direct communication between the "engravers called Blake", whether as friends or rivals, must therefore for the present remain conjectural.

VI

BLAKE'S ILLUSTRATIONS TO YOUNG'S
"NIGHT THOUGHTS"

WILLIAM BLAKE, in the year 1795, was living at Hercules
Buildings, Lambeth. For eight years he had been labouring at the composition and decoration of his series of books in
"illuminated printing", in which the text and designs were
etched on copper plates, the prints from these being then colour-
printed or painted by hand with ordinary water-colour. The
idea of combining text and decoration was, indeed, far from
new, and had been carried out in past ages in innumerable
illuminated manuscripts, though it had fallen into disuse since
the invention of printing more than three hundred years before.
Blake had unhesitatingly rejected the ordinary mode of printing, and had evolved a method which, in some of its technical
details, was entirely new. It is probable that his first experiments
were made in 1788 with the tiny plates of the brief didactic
works, *There is No Natural Religion* and *All Religions are One*.
In 1789, having gained in skill and confidence, he began to
make the twenty-eight plates of the *Songs of Innocence*. During
the next six years he executed eight more books, including *The
Marriage of Heaven and Hell*, *Songs of Innocence and of Experience*, *Europe* and *America*. The tentative beginnings of
There is No Natural Religion had proved to be the root from
which Blake's genius had grown and flowered, until in the pages
of *America*, on a scale many times larger than that of his first

attempts, he had rivalled in beauty the manuscripts of mediaeval times, and surpassed most of them in imaginative power. The colouring of the earlier copies of the *Songs of Innocence* is simple and even pallid in effect. In the later books he gave freer rein to his instinct for magnificence of colouring. This did not reach its climax until many years later, during the period 1815–20, when he was colouring superb examples of *Europe*, *America*, *Jerusalem* and other books; but by 1795 the tendency was becoming evident.

No doubt Blake's sanguine temperament had filled his mind with rosy dreams of selling hundreds of copies of his illuminated books. He was to be his own printer and publisher, and so was to obtain an easy means of livelihood while achieving the recognition that his genius desired and the propagation of the doctrines by which mankind was to be redeemed. Disappointment, however, was to be his lot. His books were sold in such small numbers that in more than one instance only a single copy is now known to have survived. It was becoming clear, therefore, by 1795 that public favour must be sought by some different means. Hitherto he had illustrated and printed only his own poems, with a success which posterity has now no hesitation in acclaiming. At the same time he had made original copper-plate engravings for only two works by other writers, namely a frontispiece for Thomas Commins's *Elegy set to Music*, 1786, a sentimental and insipid ballad, and six plates for Mary Wollstonecraft's *Original Stories from Real Life*, 1791. This and other work as journeyman engraver had brought him into relationship with some of the publishers, but whether the idea of enlarging the scope of his scheme of book decoration to include the poems of other writers originated in his own brain or another's, there is now no means of determining with certainty. Since his own compositions had failed to attract any attention, perhaps Blake wished to try the effect of a fine edition of the work of some popular favourite, putting grand marginal decorations on almost every page. If it were of a large enough size, it could scarcely fail to make some impression on the minds of his contemporaries. Certainly no scheme could seem grandiose enough to appal his imagination. In 1795 his artistic exuberance was at its height; not only were there his own illuminated books as evidence of his pre-eminence, but he had also made the series of stupendous colour-prints, including "Nebuchadnezzar", "Newton", "God Creating Adam", and a number of paintings stood to his credit. It is difficult to believe, however, that Blake's undirected impulse would have seized upon the *Night Thoughts* of Dr. Edward Young as suitable material on which to exercise his powers of illustration, though it is possible that he had chanced to read Young's prose work entitled *Conjectures on Original Composition*, which was first published in 1759. This contains many sentences which Blake must strongly have approved, such as: "Genius often then deserves most to be praised when it is most sure to be condemned; that is, when its excellence, from mounting high, to weak eyes is quite out of sight"; or again: "So boundless are the bold excursions of the human mind, that, in the vast void beyond real existence, it can call forth shadowy beings and unknown worlds, as numerous, as bright, and perhaps as lasting, as the stars . . . when such an ample area for renowned adventure in original attempts lies before us, shall we be as mere leaden pipes, conveying to the present age small streams of excellence from its grand reservoir in antiquity, and those, too, perhaps, muddied in the past?"

The *Night Thoughts* had been published in nine parts, or *Nights*, in the years 1742–45, and they had soon achieved an immense popularity which it is not easy at the present day to understand. The language has a pompous quality that only partially cloaks the lack of profundity in the thoughts expressed. Fewer, perhaps, of the present generation have read the book than have enjoyed an irreverent charade illustrating the letter Y—an elderly figure in spectacles and nightcap seated with forefinger to forehead in semi-darkness. Nevertheless Young's poetry has earned the admiration of one of the greatest of modern critics,[1] and it is possible that he may yet share in the fashionable reinstatement of the great figures of the Augustan age of literature.

In 1795 the eighteenth century had not yet been passed, so that the flavour of the *Night Thoughts* may be supposed to have been still palatable. Clearly Richard Edwards, publisher and bookseller, of 142 Bond Street, was of this opinion. Blake had not, as far as is known, done any work before this for Edwards; but when the two men met, their ideas from their different standpoints seemed good to one another, the artist eager to exercise his talents, the publisher anxious to turn this new-found genius to good commercial account. It may be guessed that Henry Fuseli acted as intermediary. Already for some years he had been Blake's friend and admirer, and had found him "damned good to steal from". He also had a far wider acquaintance than the more eccentric Blake among the literary and artistic figures of his time. When the idea of adorning Young's *Night Thoughts* with marginal designs had once been launched, Blake no doubt worked at it with feverish energy. His work began to be talked about, and some of the echoes of these conversations may be heard in the pages of the diary written by the landscape painter, Joseph Farington, R.A. On February 19,

[1] George Saintsbury, in *A Short History of English Literature*, pp. 560, 561.

1796, he notes that "West, Cosway, and Humphrey spoke warmly of the designs of Blake the engraver, as works of extraordinary genius and imagination. Smirke differed in opinion, from what he had seen; so do I." Later, on June 24, 1796, he records several facts of interest: "Fuseli called on me last night and sat till 12 o'clock. He mentioned Blake, the Engraver, whose genius and invention have been much spoken of. Fuseli has known him several years and thinks he has a good deal of invention, but that 'fancy is the end and not a means in his designs'. He does not employ it to give novelty and decoration to regular conceptions, but the whole of his aim is to produce singular shapes and odd combinations.

"Blake has undertaken to make designs and to encircle the letter-press of each page of Young's 'Night Thoughts'. Edwards, the Bookseller, of Bond Street, employs him, and has the letter-press of each page laid down on a large half-sheet of paper. There are about 900 pages. Blake asked 100 guineas for the whole. Edwards said that he could not afford to give more than 20 guineas, for which Blake agreed. Fuseli understands that Edwards proposes to select about 200 from the whole, and to have that number engraved as decorations for a new edition."

In these sentences lies the first indication of the immense scale on which Blake was working and of the minute scale on which he was to receive his reward. The scheme seems almost to obey the law of inverse squares—a principle which might have deterred a more worldly artist; but Blake was no doubt thinking, as always, more of his artistic fame than of his pecuniary reward, and his faith in his own powers carried him forward.

The pages of the first editions of the *Night Thoughts*, 1742–1745, were taken as the centre of each design. These pages were

inlaid, out of centre, toward the top and left-hand margin, in
sheets of Whatman drawing paper, which have the date 1794 in
the watermark. This date indicates that the pages were probably
made up early in 1795, when the paper manufactured during
the previous year was still being sold. The Whatman sheet was
then itself inlaid in an edging of stronger paper, on which was
drawn a ruled and tinted framework. The whole page thus constituted measures 21 × 16 inches. Blake's designs to the number
of 537 appear to have been drawn with a brush in Indian ink
and were then coloured with a varying degree of elaboration.
The intense application with which Blake worked is shewn by
the fact that this immense number of water-colour drawings
was completed and forty-three of them were engraved on copper
in less than two years, so that the first instalment of the printed
work was ready for publication in the autumn of 1797. The engraved plates bear dates ranging from June 21, 1796, to March
22, 1797, so that the time taken seems to have been about
equally divided between the water-colour drawings and the
engravings.

The publisher prepared the way by issuing early in 1797 the
following prospectus:[1]

EDWARDS'S
MAGNIFICENT EDITION
OF
YOUNG'S NIGHT THOUGHTS

Early in JUNE will be published, by subscription, part the first of a
splendid edition of this favourite work, elegantly printed, and illustrated with forty very spirited engravings from original drawings by
BLAKE.

[1] Transcribed from a copy which was in the possession of Mr. P. J. Dobell in 1914.

ILLUSTRATIONS TO YOUNG'S "NIGHT THOUGHTS"

These engravings are in a perfectly new style of decoration, surrounding the text which they are designed to elucidate.

The work is printed in atlas-sized quarto, and the subscription for the whole, making four parts, with one hundred and fifty engravings, is five guineas;—one to be paid at the time of subscribing, and one on the delivery of each part;—The price will be considerably advanced to non-subscribers.

Specimens may be seen at Edwards's, No. 142 New Bond Street; at Mr. Edwards's, Pall-Mall; and at the Historic Gallery, Pall-Mall: where subscriptions are received.

This fine "atlas quarto" consists of fifty-six separate leaves, printed on both sides, and forty-three of the pages have a large engraved design surrounding the text. This part includes only the first four "Nights" of the poem. A prefatory "Advertisement", dated December 22, 1796, declares that "no apology can be necessary for offering to the publick an embellished edition of an English classick, or for giving to the great work of Young some of those advantages of dress and ornament which have lately distinguished the immortal productions of Shakespeare and Milton". The publisher, it is stated, though "not uninfluenced by professional, acted also under the impulse of higher motives", seeking to make the arts "subservient to the purposes of religion". "In every page the reader finds his attention held captive by poetry in its boldest and most successful exertion: everywhere is his imagination soothed with pleasing, or enlarged with grand imagery: everywhere does he see fancy binding flowers round the altar of truth, while reason in awful pomp is presenting her sacrifice to heaven." After much more in the same vein, the writer asserts that the publisher "has shrunk from no expence in the preparing" of the book. "It has been regarded by him, indeed, not as a speculation of advantage, but as an indulgence of inclination—as an undertaking in which fondness and partiality would not permit him to be curiously accurate in adjusting the estimate of profit and loss." The more curious accuracy of the present day cannot help noticing that Blake had been paid at the rate of about ninepence for each of his water-colour designs, with, probably, an additional guinea for the engraving of each plate. In spite of this, the writer of the Advertisement considers that "of the merit of Mr. Blake it is unnecessary to speak", though he adds that "to the eyes of the discerning it need not be pointed out; and while a taste for the arts of design shall continue to exist, the original conception, and the bold and masterly execution of this artist cannot be unnoticed or unadmired". This ingenious, if disingenuous, preface is attributed by Alexander Gilchrist to Blake's friend, Fuseli. It seems far more probable that it was written by Edwards himself. The leaf of "Explanations of the engravings" at the end may have been compiled by Fuseli, for it was certainly not written by Blake.

Unhappily the literary and artistic public of 1797 failed to appreciate the moral exaltation predicted for them by the writer of the preface as they contemplated Young in the embrace of Blake. No contemporary reviews of the book have come to my notice, though some doubtless appeared; whether these were appreciative or unfavourable does not now matter. The venture was a failure, and the three later parts were never published; nor, so far as is known, were the plates for them ever engraved. Blake's disappointment must have been intense, but his mind was not yet touched with the bitterness and resentment that filled it in later years, so that he was probably able to find consolation enough by turning to other work. Almost immediately afterwards, indeed, he embarked on a somewhat similar series of a hundred designs for Gray's poems. These he made no attempt to publish, instead giving the volume to Mrs. Anna Flaxman as a token of gratitude to her husband for his good offices in introducing him to William Hayley.

It must be admitted that contemporary judgement, based on the merits of the engravings alone, was not far wrong. Blake's inspiration was weighed down by his technique, which still adhered to the conventions learned during his apprenticeship. Although he expresses much beauty of line, the general effect is arid and monotonous. The designs cover too large an area to be able to keep more than a part of the emotional content with which they left Blake's mind. A few copies were painted with water-colour by Blake or by his wife, but even these, though very splendid, remain somewhat unsatisfying.

The two enormous volumes containing the water-colour designs passed into the possession of Richard Edwards, whose signature appears on the fly-leaf of the first volume. Some correspondence concerning them was given to me by the late James Bain in 1925, and from this it appears that Richard Edwards afterwards sold them to his brother, Thomas Edwards of Halifax, in whose family they remained until 1874. In that year they were put into the hands of an agent, Thomas Birtwhistle, a stationer of Halifax, by whom they were brought to London in April; they were then to be seen "any morning before 11 at Anderton's Hotel, Fleet Street". On June 3, 1874, Birtwhistle wrote to James Bain, bookseller, of the Haymarket: "The owner of Blake is away but has left the sale of the Book in my hands. I could not without writing him take your price, but if you think fit to say 425£ I can make it satisfactory. It is very likely if I write he may hold out for the other 25£, as he has a great opinion of the work and is in no need of cash." The bargain was brought to a satisfactory conclusion and the books became the property of James Bain.[1] They were destined to remain for many years at his shop in the Haymarket, partly perhaps because their owner liked them too much to be willing to part from them easily, partly because they served as a centre of attraction for many customers who might otherwise have gone elsewhere to buy their books. Eventually, however, a worthy purchaser was found in the person of the late Marsden J. Perry, an American bibliophile, who in 1908 disposed of his Blake collection to William Augustus White of New York, already the owner of a large collection of Blake's illuminated books. Not long before his death in 1927 Mr. White gave them to his daughter, Mrs. Frances White Emerson, who generously presented them in the following year to the Print Room of the British Museum.

While Alexander Gilchrist was writing his *Life of Blake*, published in 1863, the drawings for *Night Thoughts* were still out of sight at Halifax. When they had been brought to London in 1874, their fame soon spread, for they were a marvellous and unexpected discovery for the slowly growing band of critics, connoisseurs and artists who were helping to raise Blake's name out of the obscurity into which it had fallen. J. Comyns Carr was one of the critics who soon afterwards expressed his admiration for the designs, and his articles in the *Cornhill* (1875) and *Belgravia* (1876) contained the first descriptions of them that were published.

[1] At some time during Bain's ownership a set of reproductions of the water-colours seems to have been projected. Messrs. Francis Edwards of Marylebone High Street recently had a lithographic full-size reproduction of No. 191 of the series, and in my collection is a coloured version of this design in miniature, in which the page of Young's text is replaced by a statement that it is a "specimen of Blake's Designs in illustration of Young's Night Thoughts. Being a reproduction, on a reduced scale, of No. 191 of the original set of Five hundred and thirty-seven Water-colour Drawings." Nothing further, however, was heard of this. No reproductions were made until 1927, when 500 copies of a set of thirty were printed by the Harvard University Press for the Fogg Museum of Art, Cambridge, Mass., with an introduction by the present writer.

ILLUSTRATIONS TO YOUNG'S "NIGHT THOUGHTS"

The volumes were included in the exhibition held at the Burlington Fine Arts Club in 1876, and a few years later a large number of the designs were described by Frederic Shields, the descriptions being printed in 1880 as an appendix to the second edition of Gilchrist's *Life*. Since that time many students of Blake's work have seen them at Bain's shop or at Mr. White's house, or, more recently, on exhibition at the British Museum, and the verdict has been unanimous that, although unequal, as is to be expected in so immense a series, the designs as a whole take a high place in the full range of Blake's artistic output. Five of them are reproduced here (Plates 16-20).

Very many are of great beauty, and some of them shew Blake's imagination working at its highest level, while embodying much of his own symbolism. On a first consideration it might seem strange that Blake should have solved so successfully the problem of illustrating Young's elusive thoughts. But actually few books could have served him better, for, as Comyns Carr wrote in 1876, "the poet says so much and means so little", that the artist is left with the widest possible range for the selection of his subjects. He may remain with Young on earth and illustrate quite literally some ordinary incident; he may seize an empty simile and give it, to the astonishment of its creator, a vivid corporeal existence; he may catch the merest breath of an allusion and, flying out far beyond the world of the bewildered poet, clothe it in the airy graces of his imagination until it assumes a beauty undreamt of while it remained in the realm of words; or he may take a vague metaphor and embody it in a design of terrifying grandeur which it had wholly missed in its original setting. All these things Blake has done many times over. He has taken the clay of Young's mind and with deft fingers has moulded it into the image of true poetry.

VII

BLAKE AND THE WEDGWOODS

D R. ERASMUS DARWIN, F.R.S., of Lichfield, grandfather of Charles Darwin, is not now regarded as a poet of distinction; yet his poem *The Botanic Garden*, the second part of which is entitled "The Loves of the Plants", is fairly well known for various reasons, one being the association of the book with the names of Josiah Wedgwood and William Blake. "The Loves of the Plants", although it is called Part II, was published first, as a quarto volume, in 1789, and in this edition it is a very scarce book. Part I, "The Economy of Vegetation", was published two years later, in 1791, and is usually associated with the second or third edition of "The Loves of the Plants". Both volumes contain a number of engravings, one of those in Part I being an engraving by Blake after a wash drawing by his friend, Henry Fuseli, entitled "The Fertilization of Egypt". Blake did not engrave directly from Fuseli's work, but made another wash drawing for himself containing additional features. The two drawings may be seen together to-day in the Print Room of the British Museum. In the engraving the dog-headed Anubis stands astride the Nile with his arms raised towards the Dog-star. In the background, the spirit of the river, a winged and bearded figure, hovers with outspread arms. This figure, a characteristic product of Blake's mind, is not shown in Fuseli's drawing, and a peculiar musical instrument known as a *cistum*, lying beside the left foot of Anubis, is not in either drawing.

Blake, however, signed the plate only as engraver, the invention being ascribed to Fuseli. Four other plates in the same volume give representations of the figures on the Portland Vase, the now famous Roman funeral vessel of deep blue glass, decorated with figures in opaque white glass. It had recently been purchased by the Duke of Portland from the Barberini family for a thousand guineas, and very skilful replicas had been made at Etruria by Josiah Wedgwood. The four unsigned plates in Dr. Darwin's volume illustrate one side of the whole vase (Plate 21), the designs in the two compartments (one on either side), and those on the bottom and the handles. They are somewhat coarsely executed, in the dot-and-lozenge technique used by Basire and his pupils, but give an excellent idea of the design of the vase. In my *Bibliography of Blake* published by the Grolier Club of New York in 1921, I noted that "the engravings of the Portland Vase ... are unsigned, but are in my opinion certainly by Blake; the style of engraving is typical of his work, and this attribution is supported by the fact that the reduced engravings of the same subject in the octavo edition of 1799 were engraved (and signed) by him". In 1930 this attribution was fully confirmed by a letter discovered by Mr. C. W. Thomas of the University of Wisconsin among the papers of the Darwin family. This letter [1] was written in July 1791 to Dr. Erasmus Darwin by Joseph Johnson, publisher of *The Botanic Garden*, and is as follows:

LONDON, *July 23, 1791*

DEAR SIR,

It is not the expence of *purchasing* Bartolozzi's plates that is any object; they *cannot be copied* without Hamilton's consent, being protected by act of parlt.

Blake is certainly capable of making an exact copy of the vase, I

---

[1] First printed in a letter which I wrote to the Editor of *The Times Literary Supplement*, July 3, 1930.

believe more so than Mr. B., if the vase were lent him for that purpose, & I see no other way of its being done, for the drawing he had was very imperfect—this you will determine on consulting Mr. Wedgwood, & also whether it should be copied as before, or reduced & brought into a folding plate.

I have no wish in this case but to do what you desire. It is not advisable to publish before the winter, yet I will do it as soon as the work is ready if you desire it.

The reason Mr. H. assigns for not allowing his plates to be copied is that he is a considerable sum out of pocket, the sale not having indemnified him for his expences.

I believe that if Dr. P. had been found by the high-church mob he would have been murdered. We hope that part of his library and some Ms. have been saved from the wreck by the activity of his son & some of his friends.

I am Sr.,

Yr. obedt.,

J. JOHNSON

I could wish for particular instructions for the engraver.

It seems certain, therefore, that Blake obtained access to the Portland Vase itself, or had the loan of a Wedgwood replica, during the autumn of 1791. The plates were rapidly completed and were published, according to the imprints, on December 1 of the same year. Blake did not, so far as is known, have any direct dealings with either Darwin or Wedgwood at this time. Joseph Johnson, however, was his close friend, and had employed him constantly for book illustrations since 1780. In 1791 he had intended to publish Blake's poem *The French Revolution*, but only the first part of this has survived, and that only in a single copy, probably a proof. Johnson's reference to Dr. Priestley's misfortunes at the end of his letter is characteristic, for he was the friend of many of the more rebellious spirits of his time besides Blake.

Mr. Thomas, when he communicated Johnson's letter to me, remarked that he had previously been struck by the resemblance between these engravings of the Portland Vase and Michelangelo's figures on the Medici tomb at Florence. Blake's early admiration for Michelangelo is very well known, and the influence is at work in his mind even when his hand is tracing the outlines of the Portland Vase.

.   .   .   .   .

Although the engravings done for Dr. Darwin in 1791 are unlikely to have brought Blake into direct relationship with Josiah Wedgwood the elder, it has long been known that Blake must have had dealings with one of the younger Wedgwoods some twenty-five years later, about the year 1816. The existence of eighteen plates of Wedgwood ware drawn and engraved by Blake has been recorded by more than one authority. A set of proofs of the engravings was in the collection of John Linnell and is now in the Print Room at the British Museum. A set of four earlier proofs, one with a watermark in the paper dated 1816, is also in the Print Room, and four proofs are in the collection of Mr. W. Graham Robertson. The latter were formerly in the possession of Blake's friend, Frederick Tatham, who wrote on one of them the following note:

Mr. Flaxman introduced Blake to Mr. Wedgwood. The Designs of the Pottery were made by Mr. Flaxman and engraved by Blake for some work. Wedgwood's last sale of pottery was about 35 or 37 years ago when I purchased several specimens. These were white that I purchased and were of very elegant shapes, some too elegant for use.

These proofs were probably known to Gilchrist, who attributed the work to the years 1781–83, when Blake first made Flaxman's acquaintance; but the date 1816 in the paper seemed to shew that the engravings were really made at a much later time in

Blake's life. No information concerning his later relations with the Wedgwoods, or the catalogue for which the engravings of pottery were presumed to have been made, was to be found in the books on Wedgwood and his wares. Investigation, however, of the mass of records preserved in the Wedgwood Museum at Etruria, made at my request by Mr. John Cook, the Curator, in 1926, produced interesting results. These were placed at my disposal by the late Frank Wedgwood, who also gave me a complete set of the engravings (Plates 22 and 23).

Blake's dealings with the firm were probably begun during the first half of the year 1815. He had sent a preliminary drawing by July, and a copy of an answering letter from Josiah Wedgwood the younger is the earliest record that has been found; it is as follows:

ETRURIA, *29 July, 1815*

Sir,—I return the drawing you have been so good to send me, which I entirely approve in all respects. I ought to have mentioned when the Terrine was sent you that the hole for the ladle in the cover should not be represented & which you will be so good to omit in the engraving.

I presume you would make a drawing of each article that is to be engraved, & if it will be agreeable to you to complete the drawings before the engraving is begun, I think it may enable me to make the best arrangement of the articles on the copper plates, but if this is not quite as agreeable to you as going on with the drawing & engraving together, I will only beg you to make two or three drawings, & I will in that case in the mean time consider of the arrangement. I have directed a Terrine to be sent you, presuming you will prefer having only one vessell at a time. If you would have more, be so good as to let Mr. Mowbray at my house know, who has a list of more articles.

I am, Sir,
Your mo. obt. svt.,
JOSIAH WEDGWOOD

Mr. Blake, 17 South Molton St.

71

BLAKE AND THE WEDGWOODS

Blake's error in representing the hole for the ladle in the Terrine may have discouraged him for a time; and it was nearly seven weeks later that he wrote the following note to Wedgwood:

17 SOUTH MOLTON STREET
8 September, 1815

SIR,—I send Two more drawings with the First that I did, altered, having taken out that part which expressed the hole for the ladle.

It will be more convenient for me to make all the drawings first, before I begin Engraving them, as it will enable me also to regulate a System of working that will be uniform from beginning to end. Any remarks that you will be pleased to make will be thankfully reciev'd by, Sir,

Your humble Servant,
WILLIAM BLAKE

No more of this polite correspondence seems to have survived; but the visionary artist was now fairly launched upon his very mundane task of making the numerous drawings that Wedgwood needed. During the last five months of the year Wedgwood's London agent was providing Blake with specimens from which to work, and the following entry occurs in the records of transactions which were sent regularly to Etruria:

October 23, 1815. For Mr. Blake for designs:

China form fruit basket, without handles & stand.
oval Cream Bowl—No. 888 of Book of Drawings.
oval rose-top Soup Terrine with listel band on cover, No. 2 Book of
    Drawings.
Butter boat, 2 handles, loose stand.

Among the articles mentioned in Mr. Wedgwood's last list for Mr. Blake to make designs from are the following eight, which have been either sent to him, or set out for him, agreeably to the preceding list recd., 8th Aug.; should the patterns be meant for the same, we

of course imagine that only one of each is meant for him—if otherwise, be pleased to mention it or enquire of Mr. Wedgwood whether
any other patterns are intended than those in his list recd. the 8th
Aug.:

> oval Salad.
> square Do.
> round Do.
> new high oval sauce terrine and std.
> round cream bowl form Do   &   Do.
> low oval Butter Boat.
> new oval Do.
> Butter Boat 2 handles fixed & std.

please to mention likewise whether the oval rose-top soup terrine
with listel band on cover, palm handles, No. 5 Book of Engravings,
as noted in Mr. Wedgwood's Mem. of 29 July, is still to be sent to
Mr. Blake to make a Design from, as it appears that he recd. No. 5
Book of Drawings from us in the first Instance instead of No. 5 Book
of Engravings. If Mr. Blake is to have the latter, please to send us one
up together with the others hereon noted.

The work was now proceeding faster; and two days later Blake
sent his patient wife to fetch yet more materials:

> 25 Oct. 1815. Mrs. Blake: 1 W.H. Basin 20 in.
> 1 Nurse Lamp with bason
> top & lip 1st Size.

By December great progress had been made:

> 5 December, 1815: Mr. Blake states that he intends very soon
> sending us some of the Drawings—he has Articles sufficient to go on
> with for the present.
> 13 Decr. 1815: Mr. Blake has left a packet of Drawings (for-
> warded herewith) from some of the articles, & states he shall very
> soon have completed Designs from all that he has.

No further references to Blake have been found in the agent's
records, and it is possible that by the end of the year the task of

making the drawings had been completed. The engravings were still to be made, and it seems to be clear that these were all done during the year 1816. A set of twelve very early proofs is now at Etruria. These are again on paper dated 1816, and have many pencil notes and marks for corrections. Several of the articles illustrated had to be completely erased and others engraved in their places. Blake's eighteen plates, most of them signed *Blake d. & sc.*, illustrated altogether 185 excellent examples of Wedgwood's pottery, all designed for domestic purposes: none of them deserve Tatham's stricture, "too elegant for use". The reward that Blake received for his work has not been ascertained with certainty, but Wedgwood's ledgers show under the date November 11, 1816, the entry:

William Blake, Engraver, London, £30 on account of engraving.

No other entry has been found, so that this may represent the whole amount that was paid.

The engravings are skilfully executed, but even Blake could not be expected to invest domestic utensils with much of his own feeling. The finished plates do not appear to have been included in any catalogue distributed by Wedgwood's to their customers, but to have been intended only for their own use. The whole set consists of thirty-one prints, the last thirteen not being executed by Blake. Numbers nineteen and twenty are signed by J. T. Wedgwood; the remainder are unsigned. Complete sets have survived only at Etruria. One set, printed in 1820 (now in my possession), was stitched into wrappers of rough brown paper and provided with a manuscript index. Other sets, printed in 1838 and 1840, show many alterations, and various plates have been added. By 1838 an index had been printed. Eight of Blake's copper-plates have actually survived to the present day, but they have been altered and partly re-engraved. In the centre of one of them Blake's figure has been erased and a "Wedge bed pan" has been put in its place.

It cannot be pretended that this recently discovered letter from Blake is possessed of any literary merit. Its biographical interest, however, is considerable. No letter of his written between the years 1809 and 1818 was hitherto known to exist. After the failure of his exhibition in 1809 he lived for ten years in a state of extraordinary obscurity, and the extant records of his life are limited to the barest hints. It is known, however, that he elaborated during 1815 three or four very splendid copies of his illuminated books and that the composition of his supreme symbolic work, *Jerusalem*, was proceeding at this time. These new records of the Wedgwood episode afford a glimpse of how the artist-poet provided some of the necessities of life. The plates of *Jerusalem* are temporarily laid aside and Blake is earning his bread in a room littered with *terrines*, *salads* and *butter-boats*.

VIII

"A DESCRIPTIVE CATALOGUE"

Blake's exhibition of his own pictures, held in the shop of his brother James in Broad Street, Golden Square, in 1809, has for long been one of the best-known events in his life, and one of the most frequently described. The exhibition was patronized by few visitors, but these few included Charles Lamb, Robert Southey, Seymour Kirkup and Crabb Robinson, whose remarks on it, particularly those of Crabb Robinson, have provided an unusually bright illumination of the incident—bright, that is, for any event at this period of Blake's life, notable in the main for its numerous dark places. Our knowledge of the exhibition is further extended by the existence of Blake's *Descriptive Catalogue*, in which he described and commented, sometimes at considerable length, on the nine frescoes and seven water-colour drawings which he chose to shew.

This catalogue was first reprinted with Gilchrist's *Life* in 1863, and was given again in the Nonesuch editions of Blake's writings, 1925 and 1927, the first of these containing reproductions of all the pictures, eleven in number, traced at the present time. Most writers on Blake have quoted from the *Catalogue* which, as Miss Mona Wilson has said in her *Life of Blake*, "is not merely a commentary on the sixteen exhibits; it is a manifesto eulogizing Raphael and Michael Angelo at the expense of Titian and Correggio, Rubens and Rembrandt" (*Life*, 1927, p. 207). The opening date of the exhibition is fixed by

76

the existence of a single-leaf typographical advertisement (Plate 24), which Blake has dated by hand, May 15, 1809, and in the *Catalogue* itself he announced that it would close on September 29. Only a single example of the advertisement leaf is known to exist, and this is now in the Bodleian Library (acquired in 1893). Gilchrist mentioned an example then (1863) in the possession of Alex. C. Weston, but this has not been traced farther than the Burlington Fine Arts Club Blake Exhibition in 1876. It was stated to bear the same date in Blake's hand and to be directed to Ozias Humphry, the miniaturist, with whom Blake corresponded. This may be identical with the copy now in the Bodleian. It has been said that another is in the library of the Royal Academy, but a recent search there has shewn this to be an error. The only "copy" to be found there is a manuscript made by J. H. Anderdon, perhaps from the original now in the Bodleian, and inserted in his extra-illustrated set of the Royal Academy catalogues.

With this relatively large amount of information about the exhibition already available, it is all the more surprising that it should have been possible to announce in 1942 the discovery of further printed matter relating to it. In the course of work on a catalogue of Blake's pictures and drawings, Mr. Ruthven Todd noticed that when the painting of "The Canterbury Pilgrims" was sold with the Thomas Butts collection at Foster's auction rooms in 1853 it was stated in the sale catalogue to be accompanied by "the artist's explanations". The lot was bought by Sir William Stirling Maxwell for 10 guineas, and inquiries addressed to his son, Sir John Stirling Maxwell, who still owns the picture, resulted in the loan of a small volume containing a bound copy of *A Descriptive Catalogue* together with a printed leaf, hitherto unrecorded, advertising the *Catalogue*. The follow-

77

ing description of this leaf is published by kind permission of the owner.

The leaf measures 13·9 × 16·5 cm., and has been folded down the centre for insertion in the book. (The sheet on which it has been mounted bears a watermark date 1820.) The text runs as follows (Plate 25):

A DESCRIPTIVE CATALOGUE

OF

B L A K E's E X H I B I T I O N,

At No. 28, Corner of

BROAD-STREET,

GOLDEN-SQUARE.

THE grand Style of Art restored; in FRESCO, or Water-colour | Painting, and England protected from the too just imputation of | being the Seat and Protectress of bad (that is blotting and blurring) | Art.

In this Exhibition will be seen real Art, as it was left us by | *Raphael* and *Albert Durer, Michael Angelo,* and *Julio Romano;* stripped | from the Ignorances of *Rubens* and *Rembrandt, Titian* and *Correggio;*

· BY WILLIAM BLAKE.

The Descriptive Catalogue, Price 2s. 6d. containing Mr. B's Opinions and Deter- | minations on Art, very necessary to be known by Artists and Connoisseurs of | all Ranks. Every Purchaser of a Catalogue will be entitled, at the time of | purchase, to view the Exhibition.

These Original Conceptions on Art, by an Original Artist, are Sold only at the | Corner of BROAD STREET. | *Admittance to the Exhibition 1 Shilling; an Index to the Catalogue gratis.* |

[double rule] | Printed by Watts & Bridgewater, Southmolton-street.

78

"A DESCRIPTIVE CATALOGUE"

In this advertisement Blake expressed his prejudices against the art of Rubens and Rembrandt, Titian and Correggio, and in favour of Raphael and Albert Durer, Michelangelo and Julio Romano, prejudices due largely to his own lack of familiarity with the pictures of the artists he condemns. His views, shewing a remarkable degree both of ignorance and insight, are developed at considerable length in the *Descriptive Catalogue*. His reference to "bad (that is blotting and blurring) Art" is also repeated in the *Catalogue*, where under Number VI, "A Spirit vaulting from a cloud to turn and wind a fiery Pegasus—Shakespeare", he writes: "This picture was done many years ago, and was one of the first Mr. B. ever did in Fresco; fortunately or rather providentially he left it unblotted and unblurred, although molested continually by blotting and blurring demons; but he was also compelled to leave it unfinished for reasons that will be shewn in the following."

In the other advertisement leaf it was announced, "Admittance 2s. 6d. each Person a descriptive Catalogue included". In the newly discovered leaflet it is stated that the Catalogue costs 2s. 6d., and that, "Every purchaser . . . will be entitled, at the time of purchase, to view the Exhibition". But, lest this charge should seem excessive, the last line of the advertisement adds, "Admittance to the Exhibition 1 Shilling; an Index to the Catalogue gratis". Even this inducement was insufficient to attract many patrons, for the exhibition received little or no attention except for a virulent attack in Leigh Hunt's paper, *The Examiner*, published on September 17, not long before it closed. Thomas Butts was, it seems, the only purchaser of any of the pictures exhibited, seven of them, and probably more, being afterwards in his collection.

The two advertisement leaves appear to have been printed in

the same shop in South Molton Street, where Blake also had his single apartment, though the name of the firm is given as "Watts and Co." on one, and as "Watts and Bridgewater" on the other. The *Descriptive Catalogue* itself was printed by D. N. Shury, Soho. The offer of "an Index to the Catalogue gratis" suggests that there may be yet another separate leaf to be discovered, though this would probably be merely an off-print of the index given on the fourth leaf of the *Catalogue*.

Full bibliographical details of the first advertisement and the *Catalogue* are to be found in my *Bibliography of Blake*, Grolier Club, New York, 1921. Since that date, however, a number of additional copies of the *Catalogue* have come to light, and this opportunity may be taken of providing a revised census of copies. Eighteen copies are described. Some of these have the address of the exhibition added on the title-page in Blake's hand (Plate 26), and a correction in the text on page 64. The careful addition of the address to so many copies, and the emphasis on the address in the two advertisement leaves, suggests that Blake was fearful lest its not being well enough known should discourage visitors. It is interesting to notice that Blake still had a spare copy of the *Catalogue* by him as late as 1824, which he gave to young Frederick Tatham in June of that year.

(A) British Museum Reading Room. Acquired March 29, 1864. Press-mark C.31, h.21. Bound in morocco, gilt, 18 × 11 cm. No MS. addition on title-page.

(B) British Museum Print Room. Inscribed "Presented by William Smith Esq., 1856". Bound in cloth, morocco back, 18 × 10·5 cm. With MS. addition on title-page.

(C) G. L. Keynes. Probably to be identified with a copy offered by Messrs. Low Brothers, Birmingham, for 7s. 6d. in a catalogue issued in February 1915. It was sold in 1916 by Messrs. Maggs Brothers for £13 to the late William Bateson, F.R.S., who gave it to the present owner in 1922. Stitched in its original blue wrappers, uncut, 19 × 11·5 cm. With MS. addition on title-page, and correction on p. 64. This seems to be the only copy which has remained, except for some repairs to the wrapper, exactly as it was issued in 1809.

(D) H. E. Huntington Library, California. From the T. G. Arthur library, sold at Sotheby's, July 15, 1914 (lot 45, G. D. Smith, £24 : 10s.). Bound in brown morocco, gilt edges, by Bedford.

(E) William Cowan copy, sold at Sotheby's, Dec. 4, 1912 (lot 849, Quaritch, £4). Not traced. Bound in morocco, gilt, 19 × 11 cm. With MS. addition on title-page.

(F) Beckford-Hamilton Palace copy. Sold at Sotheby's, July 4, 1882 (Quaritch, £9). Traded to America, and bought later by G. D. Smith who sold it to Mr. Felix Isman. Sold again in 1932 to Dr. A. S .W. Rosenbach, from whom it was acquired by Mr. Chauncey B. Tinker, Yale University. Bound in green morocco, gilt, marbled edges. With MS. addition on title-page, and correction on p. 64. Exhibited at the Grolier Club, 1905 (no. 36 in the catalogue).

(G) Fitzwilliam Museum, Cambridge, presented by the late Charles Fairfax Murray. Bound with the original wrappers in blue morocco, gilt, 19 × 11·5 cm. With MS. addition on title-page.

(H) Bodleian Library, Oxford, bequeathed by Francis Douce in 1835. Bound in half-calf, 18 × 11 cm. With MS. addition on title-page, and correction on p. 64.

(I) Robert Balmanno copy. Afterwards in the E. W. Hooper collection, and bequeathed by Hooper to his daughter, Mrs. Greely S. Curtis, Jr., Boston, Mass. Bound with an uncoloured copy of *Songs of Innocence* (Keynes, copy U), and *The Prologue and Characters of Chaucer's Pilgrims*, 1812, 19 × 11·5 cm. The fly-leaf of the volume has a watermark dated 1818.

(J) B. B. Macgeorge copy, sold at Sotheby's, July 1, 1924 (lot 124, Dobell, £9 : 10s.). Offered by Messrs. Maggs Brothers in a catalogue in November 1924, for £21. Afterwards in the collection of Willis Vickery, and then in that of the late A. Edward Newton, sold at the Parke-Bernet Galleries, New York, April 17, 1941 (lot 149, T. J. Gannon, $275.00). Bound in red morocco, gilt edges, by Rivière. With MS. addition on title-page, and correction on p. 64. Now in the collection of Mr. Paul Mellon.

(K) Lessing J. Rosenwald. John Linnell's copy, bound with a copy of *Poetical Sketches*, and inscribed on the fly-leaf "John Linnell, 38, Porchester Terrace, Bayswater, 1846". Below is written "To James T. L., 1866", *i.e.* given by Linnell to his son, James T. Linnell. Now in the Lessing J. Rosenwald collection, Library of Congress.

(L) W. A. White copy. Bound in green morocco by Zaehnsdorf, untrimmed, with the original wrappers preserved. With MS. addition on title-page, and correction on p. 64. Sold at Sotheby's, July 14, 1895 (Quaritch, 3 gns.), and acquired by W. A. White. Bought after his death by Dr. A. S. W. Rosenbach, who disposed of it in 1929 to Mr. Lessing J. Rosenwald. Now in the Lessing J. Rosenwald Collection, Library of Congress.

(M) A. S. W. Rosenbach. From the library of Lt.-Col. W. E. Moss, sold at Sotheby's, Feb. 2, 1937 (lot 196, Rosenbach, £50). The pages, 19 × 11 cm., are inlaid throughout on larger leaves. Bound in brown morocco, gilt, by Bedford. No MS. addition on title-page.

(N) E. J. E. Tunmer, sold at Sotheby's, June 15, 1937 (lot 346, Robinson, £37). Offered for sale by Messrs. Robinson, Pall Mall, in March 1938, for £60. Acquired by Mr. Otis T. Bradley, New York. Sold at the Parke-Bernet Galleries, New York, November 6, 1944 (lot 78) and again, October 4, 1946 (lot 46). Bound in cloth, edges untrimmed.

(O) Sir John Stirling Maxwell, Bt. From the collection of Thomas Butts, sold at Foster's, June 29, 1853, with the tempera of "The Canterbury Pilgrims" (lot 93, Stirling, £10 : 10s.). Then in the collection of Sir William Stirling Maxwell and now in that of his son. Bound in red quarter-roan and cloth, with the leaflet here first described, top edges gilt, others untrimmed, 18·4 × 11 cm., bookplate of William Stirling of Keir, *i.e.* Sir William Stirling Maxwell. With MS. addition on title-page, and correction on p. 64. (The title-page is reproduced here, Plate 26.)

(P) Tatham copy. Inscribed on the title-page, in Tatham's hand, "Frederick [Ta]tham | from the Author | June 12, 1824". No inscription by Blake on the title-page and no correction on p. 64. Sold with the Phillipps collection of printed books, Sotheby's, November 25, 1946 (lot 27, Quaritch, £85). Next in the collection of Mr. Arthur Randle and resold at Sotheby's, October 1, 1948 (lot 34, Rosenbach, £95). Bound in calf, and lettered *Blake's Catalogue of Pictures*.

(Q) Inserted in the J. H. Anderdon extra-illustrated copy of the Royal Academy catalogues, now in the library of the Royal Academy, is a cutting from an undated bookseller's catalogue, offering a copy of *A Descriptive Catalogue* . . . "calf neat . . . 6s. Presentation copy from the Author and MS. Memoranda by Mr. M., &c., &c." The only "Mr. M." who would have been likely to receive a copy from Blake would appear to be Benjamin Heath Malkin, author of *A Father's Memoirs of His Child*, 1806. This cannot be identified with any copy listed above.

(R) Robert Arthington of Leeds copy, sold at Sotheby's, May 17, 1866 (lot 21, £1 : 9s.). Possibly later in the possession of A. Anderdon Weston, and to be identified with a copy described above.

(S) Charles Lamb bound his copy with Elia's *Confessions of a Drunkard*, Southey's *Wat Tyler*, and the *Poems* of Rochester and Lady Winchelsea. This volume has not been traced.

Robert Southey probably possessed a copy, and Crabb Robinson records that he purchased four, but none of these has been identified.

IX

WILLIAM BLAKE WITH CHARLES LAMB
AND HIS CIRCLE[1]

IT IS ALWAYS interesting to speculate on the contacts and re-
actions upon one another of great contemporaries, and to
wonder why this one or that could not see the merits of the
other, which to us at the distance of a hundred or two hundred
years seem so plain or even transcendent. So it has appeared
to me to be worth while to string together the rather scrappy
evidences (which are all that we possess) connecting William
Blake with some of his contemporaries, and no contemporaries
could be more appropriate for the Charles Lamb Society
than Lamb himself and some of his immediate friends and
acquaintances.

The following are some unpublished lines by Blake:

> A Woman Scaly and a Man all hairy
> Is such a match as he who dares
> Will find the woman's scales will
> scrape off the man's hairs.

These strange lines are unpublished because they have only
been recently deciphered by the late Max Plowman among the
dim pencillings found in Blake's manuscript note-book. The
lines taken by themselves sound senseless, and many would be
reluctant to accept them as the serious utterance of a great poet
and artist. Let it, however, be understood that the lines were
written down in a private notebook, most of the contents of

[1] A paper read to the Charles Lamb Society, October 9, 1943.

which were not intended for publication, so that we are really eavesdropping and violating the privacy of Blake's chamber. Nevertheless, these apparently idle words can be given meaning if they are correlated with the habit of Blake's mind and his symbolic system. The "Man all hairy" may be Orc, the Spirit of Revolt in man's nature, a personification who plays an important part in all Blake's symbolic works.[1] The "Woman Scaly" is the evil side of sex and materialism, a covering of scales being always an attribute of Blake's Satan, the opponent of the Imagination and of the world of the Spirit, which had so much more meaning and value for Blake than any of our mundane and material affairs. The words quoted express, therefore, the results of a conflict between two great opposed forces, material and spiritual, the kind of conflict with which Blake's mind was obsessed and which gave rise to much of his greatest, albeit most obscure, utterances. Orc might have won the battle against a mere scaly Satan; but a Woman Scaly, Blake feared, would scrape off the hairs of Orc, and so emasculate the Spirit of Revolt.

These new lines by Blake are quoted not for mystification, but in order to illustrate the queerness of his mind, and to emphasize the gulf that was necessarily fixed in the way of an easy understanding between Blake and a person such as the Patron Saint of the Charles Lamb Society, or between Blake and the other members of Lamb's circle.

It seems improbable that Blake was known to Lamb or most others of his circle until 1809,[2] the year in which Blake held his

---

[1] See *America*, Preludium (*Poetry and Prose*, ed. Keynes, 1939, p. 201).

[2] In 1807 Lamb's *Tales from Shakespeare* appeared in two volumes with a number of engraved plates which have been persistently attributed to Blake by generations of booksellers. These illustrations were, however, designed by William Mulready, and the technique of the engraving does not suggest Blake's work. It may be safely assumed that Blake had no hand in them.

exhibition of pictures at the house of his brother James, the hosier, 28 Broad Street, Golden Square. The exhibition was open from May until September, and Blake had high hopes that it would serve to spread his fame and obtain him the recognition that he knew he deserved. In fact it did exactly the opposite. The pictures had few visitors, and the only public notice given to it was in an article published in *The Examiner* by Robert Hunt, brother of the editor Leigh Hunt, on September 17, 1809, not long before the exhibition closed. In this article Blake is described as "an unfortunate lunatic whose personal inoffensiveness secures him from confinement", and his now celebrated *Descriptive Catalogue* was condemned as "a farrago of nonsense, unintelligibleness, and egregious vanity, the wild effusions of a distempered brain".[1] Among the few visitors was Henry Crabb Robinson, a tireless hunter of interesting characters and disseminator of literary and artistic gossip. In his well-known Diary he recalled that before writing an account of Blake for a German magazine he went to see the gallery of Blake's paintings in Carnaby Market, that is in Broad Street, Golden Square. "These paintings", he wrote, "filled several rooms of an ordinary dwelling house. The entrance was two shillings and sixpence, catalogue included. I was deeply interested by the catalogue as well as the pictures. I took four, telling the brother, I hoped he would let me come in again. He said; 'Oh, as often as you please'. I daresay such a thing had never happened before, or did afterwards." Crabb Robinson added later that he took four copies of the *Catalogue* because he "wished to send it to Germany, and to

---

[1] Hunt had also been attacking the "extravagances" of Blake's friend, Fuseli, and had indeed criticised them both in an adverse review of the edition of Blair's *Grave* illustrated by Blake. This was published in an early number of *The Examiner* (August 7, 1808) and Fuseli is there characterized as "a frantic". It was all part of a press campaign, in Mr. Edmund Blunden's view.

give a copy to Lamb and others". We may be sure that he did
not remain silent about his visit, and he particularly mentions
that at this time "I frequently saw Lamb, Hazlitt, indeed most
of my old acquaintances as well the literary as my family con-
nections". It seems fairly clear, therefore, that his interest so
volubly expressed, together with his gifts of the *Descriptive
Catalogue*, stimulated others to visit Blake's exhibition, and these
included Lamb and Robert Southey. Crabb Robinson did not
meet Blake himself until many years later in 1825, and there is
no evidence that Lamb ever met him at any time. Crabb Robinson recorded, however, that Lamb considered Blake's description
of his "Canterbury Pilgrims" "the finest criticism he had ever
read of Chaucer's poem", and Lamb himself, writing some years
later in May 1824, to the Quaker poet, Bernard Barton, gave
his own opinion as follows: "Blake is a real name, I assure you,
and a most extraordinary man if he be still living. He is the
Robert Blake [meaning William], whose wild designs accom-
pany a splendid folio edition of the Night Thoughts. . . . He
paints in water colours marvellous strange pictures, visions of his
brain, which he asserts that he has seen. They have great merit.
He has *seen* the old Welsh bards on Snowdon . . . and has
painted them from memory (I have seen his paintings). . . . His
Pictures—one in particular, the Canterbury Pilgrims (far above
Stothard's)—have great merit, but hard, dry, yet with grace. He
has written a Catalogue of them, with a most spirited criticism
on Chaucer, but mystical and full of Vision. . . . There is one
[song] to a tiger, which I have heard recited . . . which is glorious,
but alas! I have not the book; for the man is flown, whither I
know not—to Hades or a Mad House. But I must look on him
as one of the most extraordinary persons of the age. . . ." In this
same year, 1824, Lamb obtained a copy of Blake's poem, "The

BLAKE WITH LAMB AND HIS CIRCLE

Chimney Sweeper" from the *Songs of Innocence* for James Montgomery's *Chimney Sweeper's Friend and Climbing Boy's Annual*,
and regarded it as "the flower of the set" (Plate 28). Of Montgomery, Crabb Robinson wrote in 1812, "He looks like a
methodist parson, and has what Wordsworth expressed [as] the
appearance of a feeble and amiable man". This agrees with the
impression given of this sentimental poet, hymn-writer, and
journalist in the *Memoirs* of him published in 1854, where we
read, "When [Blair's] Grave was afterwards published, with
Blake's splendid illustrations, he [Montgomery] became the pos-
sessor of a copy; but, as several of the plates were hardly of such
a nature as to render the book proper to lie on a parlour table for
general inspection, he sold his copy for the subscription price; a
circumstance which he often regretted, as the death of the artist
soon afterwards rendered the work both scarce and proportion-
ately more valuable. Those persons who have once seen these
illustrations will readily recollect the print representing the angel
of the 'last trump' descending to awake the dead. . . . The solemn
absurdity of this conception, and the ingenious manner in which
it is executed, afforded Montgomery a very amusing topic of
conversation on one occasion when we were present." Nevertheless this feeble and amiable man, who could sneer so amusingly
at Blake, was not above stealing from the object of his ridicule,
for the *Climbing Boy's Annual* contains in addition to "The
Chimney Sweeper", obtained for him by Lamb, a plagiarism of
Blake's "The Dream", which is a version of the poem extended
or, as Lamb called it in his letter to Barton, "awkwardly para-
phrased from Blake". Crabb Robinson's meeting with Blake in
1825 and his subsequent cultivation of Blake's acquaintance no
doubt led to many talks on the subject with his friends, so that
Lamb would soon have been enlightened, learning that Blake's

88

first name was William, not Robert, and that he was neither dead
nor in a mad-house, but still very active, and indeed at the
culmination of his creative career in his designs for *The Book
of Job* and Dante. The final recorded incident connecting
Blake with Lamb was on January 8, 1828, when Crabb
Robinson called on Blake's widow and bought two prints of
"The Canterbury Pilgrims" for 2½ guineas each, meaning one
of them for Lamb, who actually received on May 22, 1828,
the picture he had so much admired nearly twenty years
before.

We must now go back to the year 1805, in which was published a duodecimo volume containing the inane ballads of the
poet of Eartham, William Hayley, illustrated with five engravings by Blake. The frontispiece illustrates the ballad of "The
Dog" in which the faithful Fido leaps into the water in order to
save his master, Edward, from a crocodile waiting unnoticed
beneath him (Plate 29). This book was reviewed by Robert
Southey in *The Annual Register*. He ridiculed the ballads, and
added: "The poet has had the singular good fortune to meet
with a painter capable of doing full justice to his conceptions;
and in fact when we look at the delectable frontispiece to this
volume which represents Edward starting back, Fido *volant*, and
the crocodile *rampant*, with a mouth open like a bootjack to
receive him, we know not whether most to admire the genius of
Mr. William Blake or of Mr. William Hayley." Southey concluded his review: "We could not help quoting O'Keefe's song—
Hayley-gaily gamboraly higgledy piggledy galloping draggle-
tail'd dreary dun". It was easy to ridicule Blake's pictures, but
Southey did not know the circumstances in which they were produced—Blake's genius labouring in Hayley's fetters. He would
perhaps have shewn more understanding if he could have read

Blake's epigrams jotted down in his notebook at this period to relieve his feelings:

> Of H[ayley]'s birth this was the happy lot,
> His Mother on his Father him begot,

and

> Thy Friendship oft has made my heart to ake:
> Do be my enemy for Friendship's sake.

To follow Southey's further relations with Blake we must go on to the year 1811 to attend a party at Lamb's house on July 24. Crabb Robinson is again our informant. "Returned late to Charles Lamb's. Found a very large party there. Southey had been with Blake, and admired both his designs and his poetic talents, at the same time that he held him for a decided madman. Blake, he says, spoke of his visions with the diffidence that is usual with such people, and did not seem to expect that he should be believed. He showed Southey a perfectly mad poem called *Jerusalem*—Oxford Street is in Jerusalem." It is interesting to learn from this that Robert Southey was the first member of the Lamb circle whose curiosity and interest in Blake led him to seek him out in his own surroundings. Southey had in 1811 already lived for some years at Greta Hall, Coleridge's house near Keswick, but in this year he undertook a three months' journey round England, and it was in the course of this that he visited Blake in London. Blake evidently sensed that he was the object of a somewhat patronizing curiosity, and talked with what seemed to Southey the diffidence of a diseased mind. It is much more probable that Blake gave this impression because, being accustomed to contacts with minds less intelligent and more commonplace than his own, he did not attempt to impress on his visitor a view of art and poetry which he knew would not be understood. He did not want it to be understood—this was one of Blake's great failings—and though he produced for Southey

some leaves of his great poem *Jerusalem*, then only partly com-
posed, he did so more to mystify and confound than to enlighten.
What could Southey know of the building of Golgonooza, the
City of Art and Imagination?

> What are those golden builders doing? Where was the burying place
> Of soft Ethinthus? near Tyburn's fatal Tree? is that
> Mild Zion's hill's most ancient promontory, near mournful
> Ever-weeping Paddington? is that Calvary and Golgotha
> Becoming a building of pity and compassion? Lo!
> The stones are pity, and the bricks, well wrought affections
> Enamel'd with love & kindness, & the tiles engraven gold,
> Labour of merciful hands: the beams & rafters are forgiveness:
> The mortar & cement of the work, tears of honesty: the nails
> And the screws & iron braces are well wrought blandishments
> And well contrived words, firm fixing, never forgotten,
> Always comforting the remembrance: the floors, humility,
> The cielings, devotion: the hearths, thanksgiving.
> Prepare the furniture, O Lambeth, in thy pitying looms,
> The curtains, woven tears & sighs wrought into lovely forms
> For comfort; there the secret furniture of Jerusalem's chamber
> Is wrought. Lambeth! the Bride, the Lamb's Wife, loveth thee.
> Thou art one with her & knowest not of self in thy supreme joy.
> Go on, builders in hope, tho' Jerusalem wanders far away
> Without the gate of Los, among the dark Satanic wheels.
>
> *(Jerusalem, plate 12)*

No wonder Southey was mystified and, in spite of himself, im-
pressed. The only Lamb that Blake knew was the Lamb of God,
and to him the Holy Name meant the creative imagination and
the divine world of art. His poetry was overlaid with a symbolism compounded of elements from the Celtomaniacs and the
Druidists, from the Gnostics, the Cabalists, the Hindoos, from
Jacob Boehme, and from Swedenborg. Oxford Street is mentioned in a passage on plate 38 of *Jerusalem*:

> There is in Albion a Gate of precious stones and gold
> Seen only by Emanations, by vegetations viewless:

BLAKE WITH LAMB AND HIS CIRCLE

Bending across the road of Oxford Street, it from Hyde Park
To Tyburn's deathful shades admits the wandering souls
Of multitudes who die from Earth: this Gate can not be found
By Satan's Watch-fiends, tho' they search numbering every grain
Of sand on Earth every night, they never find this gate.

This would mystify Southey as much as "mournful, ever-weeping Paddington", and he could not know that the topography of London and of the Holy Land are inextricably mixed in *Jerusalem*, both bearing a heavy burden of symbolic meaning.

Nearly twenty years after his visit to Blake, Southey described his experience to Caroline Bowles, a minor poetess, who was afterwards to become the wife of his declining years. "1 have nothing", he wrote, "of Blake's but his designs for Blair's *Grave*, which were published with the poem. His still stranger designs for his own compositions in verse were not ready for sale when I saw him, nor did I ever hear that they were so. [This evidently refers to the then unfinished *Jerusalem*, which Blake shewed him. It is significant that Blake did not apparently care to shew him any of his other earlier books, many of which could have been bought for modest sums.] Much as he is to be admired, he was at that time so evidently insane, that the predominant feeling in conversing with him, or even looking at him, could only be sorrow and compassion. His wife partook of his insanity in the same way (but more happily) as Taylor the pagan's wife caught her husband's paganism. . . . I came away from the visit with so sad a feeling that I never repeated it. . . . You could not have delighted in him—his madness was too evident, too fearful. It gave his eyes an expression such as you would expect to see in one who was possessed."

A few years after writing this letter, Southey reverted to the subject of Blake in volumes six and seven of *The Doctor*, published in 1837–47, a vast, garrulous, facetious repository of curious information. He quoted from the *Descriptive Catalogue* a piece about the now lost picture of "The Ancient Britons" and the "Mad Song" from *Poetical Sketches*, written when Blake was a boy, introducing him as "That painter of great, but insane, genius". He also related John Varley's account of how Blake painted a portrait of the Ghost of a Flea, concluding with some very trite reflections of his own. It is of interest to notice that in quoting the now famous "Mad Song" he introduced the emendation "rustling birds of dawn" for the "beds of dawn" in the printed text of the second stanza. It may be inferred that Southey used one of the copies of *Poetical Sketches* in which Blake had made this correction.[1]

We must depend again on Crabb Robinson's reporting for an opinion of Blake from one of the most interesting of Lamb's circle, William Hazlitt. On March 10, 1811, Robinson showed Hazlitt Blake's designs for Young's *Night Thoughts*, published in 1807, and reported: "He saw no merit in them as designs. I read him some of the poems. He was much struck with them and expressed himself with his usual strength and singularity. 'They are beautiful,' he said, 'and only too deep for the vulgar. He has no sense of the ludicrous, and, as to a God, a worm crawling in a privy is as worthy an object as any other, all being to him indifferent. So to Blake the Chimney Sweeper, etc. He is ruined by vain struggles to get rid of what presses on his brain—he attempts at impossibilities.' I added: 'He is like a man who lifts a burden too heavy for him; he bears it an instant, it then falls on him and crushes him'." Characteristically Hazlitt's acute mind had seized quickly on some of Blake's weak points, while admiring unfeignedly the beauty of his verse. About the year 1784

[1] See p. 31 of the present volume.

Blake had attempted a satire on contemporary society in the form of a burlesque novel known as *An Island in the Moon*, and there is certainly some fun in *The Marriage of Heaven and Hell*, but otherwise we possess little evidence that he had a well-developed sense of humour. This is not maintaining that a sense of humour is necessary for the flowering of poetic genius, and indeed it is impossible to imagine Blake allowing himself to be distracted by facetious trivialities. A deep seriousness pervaded all his thoughts and actions, and had he been a more ordinary person we might justly have complained that he took himself too seriously. Hazlitt was also right that Blake often attempted impossibilities. Had he known him better he might have added that *though* he attempted impossibilities, particularly in his pictures, he frequently succeeded. The engravings in Young's *Night Thoughts* which Crabb Robinson showed to Hazlitt are some of Blake's least successful efforts, and would not be expected to impress so good a critic. But had he seen the great series of colour prints now in the Tate Gallery, the designs for *Paradise Lost*, the *Illustrations of the Book of Job*, or the water-colours for Dante, then he must have made some concession to Blake's claims.

Crabb Robinson himself was quite unable to appreciate Blake's paintings and frankly confessed to this. On one occasion after Blake's death he was offered three of his designs for £5, but rejected them as too dear. Robinson was, indeed, himself puzzled to know why he, so logical and unimaginative, was so much interested by Blake's visionary and elusive mind, and in spite of having decided, even before they had met, that Blake was mad. The explanation must be that Robinson had convincingly detected the blend of intellect with true inspiration in Blake's poetry, and enjoyed the attempt to discover from his conversation the source and quality of his genius. It must be admitted that Blake's conversation as reported by Crabb Robinson was uncompromising in its assumption of the character of prophet and visionary. He made no concessions to his visitor's possible lack of sympathy and understanding, and talked of his strange doctrines and his visions of Voltaire and Shakespeare without any of the diffidence noted by Southey.

The subject of Blake's conversation introduces one of the most disappointing of his contacts with Lamb's circle; disappointing, that is, in the absence of any detailed account of what took place. This is Blake's meeting, or meetings, with Coleridge. In the year 1818 Charles Augustus Tulk, an eminent follower of Emmanuel Swedenborg, had lent Coleridge his copy of the *Songs of Innocence and of Experience*.[1] The exact date of this is fixed by a postscript written by Coleridge in a letter to H. F. Cary as follows:[2]

HIGHGATE, *February 6, 1818*

. . . PS. I have this morning been reading a strange publication—*viz.* Poems with very wild and interesting pictures, as swathing, etched (I suppose) but it is said printed and painted by the author, W. Blake. He is a man of Genius—and I apprehend a Swedenborgian—certainly a mystic *emphatically.* You perhaps smile at *my* calling another poet a *Mystic*; but verily I am in the very mire of common-place common-place compared with Mr. Blake, apo- or rather ana-calyptic Poet, and Painter!

When Coleridge returned the book to Tulk he wrote a letter giving an elaborate critique of the poems. He evidently thought highly of them, and marked them in order of merit. Top marks he gave to "The Little Black Boy". The whole letter is as follows:

[1] Now in the possession of Lord Rothschild, who has kindly allowed me to transcribe Coleridge's letter.

[2] *Coleridge Select Poetry and Prose* (ed. Stephen Potter, London, Nonesuch Press, 1933).

BLAKE WITH LAMB AND HIS CIRCLE

To C. A. Tulk Esqr (or Mrs. Tulk)
St. John's Lodge
Regent's Park

HIGHGATE, *Thursday evening, 1818*

Blake's Poems—I begin with my Dyspathies, that I may forget them: and have uninterrupted space for Loves and Sympathies.

Title-page and the following emblem contain all the faults of the Drawings with as few beauties as could be in the composition of a man who was capable of such faults + such beauties. The faults— despotism in symbols, amounting in the title page to the μισητέον and occasionally regular unmodified Lines of the Inanimate, sometimes as the effect of rigidity and sometimes of exosseation—like a wet tendon. So likewise the ambiguity of the Drapery. Is it a garment—or the body incised and scored out? The Limpness (= the effect of Vinegar on an egg) in the upper one of the two prostrate figures on the Title- page, and the *eye*-likeness of the twig posteriorly on the second, and the strait line down the waist-coat of pinky gold beaters' skin in the next drawing, with the I-don't-know-whatness of the countenance as if the mouth had been formed by the habit of placing the tongue, not contemptuously, but stupidly, between the lower gums and the lower jaw—these are the only *repulsive* faults I have noticed. The figure, however, of the second leaf (abstracted from the *expression* of the Countenance, given it by something about the mouth and the inter- space from the lower lip to the chin) is such as only a master, learned in his art, could produce.

N.B.—1 signifies, It gave me pleasure.
⊥ still greater.
⊥⊥ and greater still.
ө in the highest degree.
o in the lowest.

Shepherd 1 Spring 1 (last stanza ⊥)
Holy Thursday ⊥⊥   Laughing Song ⊥
Nurses Song 1   The Divine Image ө
The Lamb ⊥   The Little Black Boy ө: yea, ө + ө!
Infant Joy ⊥⊥ (n.b. for the 3 last lines I should wish "When

96

BLAKE WITH LAMB AND HIS CIRCLE

wilt thou smile", or, "O smile, O smile! I'll sing the
while"—For a Babe two days old does not, cannot, *smile*
—and Innocence and the very works of nature must go
together. Infancy is too holy a thing to be ornamented.
Echoing Green 1 (the figures 1, and of the second leaf 11).
The Cradle Song 1
The School Boy 11   Night 0
On another's Sorrow 1   A Dream?
The little Boy lost 1   (the drawing 1)
The little boy found 1   The Blossom 0
The Chimney Sweeper 0   The v. of the ancient Bard 0
Introduction 1   Earth's Answer 1
Infant sorrow 1   The Clod and the Pebble 1
The garden of Love 1   The fly 1   The Tyger 1
A little Boy lost 1   Holy Thursday 1
p. 13 [The Angel] 0   Nurse's Song 0   The little girl lost
And found (the ornaments most exquisite! the poem 1)
Chimney Sweeper in the Snow 0   To Tirzah and The
Poison Tree 1 and yet 0.   A little girl lost—0 (I would
have had it omitted—not for the want of innocence in the
poem, but by the too probable want of it in many readers).
London 1   The sick Rose 1   *The little Vagabond*—

Tho' I cannot approve altogether of this last poem and have been
inclined to think that the error which is most *likely* to beset the
Scholars of Em. Sw. is that of utterly *de*merging the Tremendous in-
compatibilities with an evil will that arise out of the essential Holiness
of the abysmal Aseity, in the Love of the eternal *Person*—and thus
giving temptation to weaker minds to sink this Love itself into *good
nature*—yet still I disapprove the mood of mind in this wild poem so
much less than I do the servile, blind-worm, wrap-rascal Scurf-coat
& *fear* of the *modern Saints* (whose whole Being is a Lie, to themselves
as well as to their Brethren) that I should laugh with good conscience
in watching a Saint of the new stamp, one of the First stars of our
eleemosynary Advertisements groaning in—wind-pipe! and with the
whites of his Eyes upraised at the *audacity* of this poem!—Anything

97

rather than *this* degradation[1] of Humanity, and there-in of the incarnate Divinity!

S. T. C.

o means that I am perplexed and have no opinion.
[1] with which how can we utter "Our Father"? [1]

A few years later, in 1826, Crabb Robinson told Dorothy Wordsworth in a letter, "Coleridge has visited Blake, and I am told talks finely about him". Three years after this, in 1829, and about eighteen months after Blake's death, an article headed "The Inventions of William Blake, Painter and Poet" appeared in the *London University Magazine*. It is unsigned, and no clue to its author has been discovered, though it is clearly by someone who knew and understood Blake well. Perhaps it was by Tulk himself who was a supporter of London University. The writer regarded Blake as a great genius, unjustly neglected by his own nation, and saw in him much hope for the future of English art. "We have a confident hope," he wrote, "that Coleridge, Blake and Flaxman are the forerunners of a more elevated and purer system, which has even now begun to take root in the breast of the English nation; they have laid a foundation for future minds—Coleridge, for the developement of a more internal philosophy—Blake and Flaxman, for a purer and

[1] Mr. J. H. Wicksteed has made the following remarks on this letter quoted by his permission: "I suggest that the full significance of this unique commentary by a unique mind does not emerge on a first reading, and that a footnote or so would be a considerable help to the average reader. I suggest, for instance, a note on the word *aseity*, which is not common enough to be in the first issue of the *Concise Oxford Dictionary*, but is adequately treated in the *Shorter Oxford Dictionary*. It is not Greek (as Atheist, Agnostic, Amoral, etc.), but Latin, *a se*, by itself, or himself, *i.e.* not proceeding from, or created by, something more basically real or essential than itself. The whole letter exhibits S. T. C. struggling to express his own penetrating mind in 'shock' response to W. B.'s, and in such a way as to be intelligible and acceptable to a good, but not outstanding, contemporary intelligence. Incidentally it fails to establish its intrinsic worth with our age just because it fails to realise the profound element of Blakean humour mingled with Blake's scathing tongue. It is Swedenborg who is almost humourless, not Blake, and S. T. C. reads W. B. in the misleading light of Swedenborg."

more ennobling sentiment in works of art." He then discusses Blake's poetry, quoting several of the *Songs* and also parts of the exquisite *Book of Thel*. Finally, in a footnote at the end, he added, "Blake and Coleridge, when in company, seemed like congenial beings of another sphere, breathing for a while on our earth; which may easily be perceived from the similarity of thought pervading their works." There we are tantalizingly abandoned, for no echo of this divine conversation has come down to us. All opinions of Coleridge's contemporaries seem to agree that he was not a good listener, but it may be that Blake's conversation was arresting enough even to break the flow of Coleridge's eloquence.

It would be possible to write an essay on the similarities between Coleridge and Blake; possible, that is, for one who knows Coleridge's mind and writings more intimately than I do. There is, however, one passage in Coleridge to which Walter Pater drew attention owing to its being comparable to one of Blake's most famous designs. It is the passage in *The Ancient Mariner* describing the re-inspiriting of the dead men on the ship:

> The helmsman steered, the ship moved on;
> Yet never a breeze up-blew;
> The mariners all 'gan work the ropes,
> Where they were wont to do;
> They raised their limbs like lifeless tools—
> We were a ghastly crew.

> 'I fear thee, ancient Mariner!'
> Be calm, thou Wedding-Guest!
> 'Twas not those souls that fled in pain,
> Which to their corses came again,
> But a troop of spirits blest:

> For when it dawn'd—they dropped their arms,
> And cluster'd round the mast;
> Sweet sounds rose slowly through their mouths,
> And from their bodies pass'd.

Around, around, flew each sweet sound,
Then darted to the Sun;
Slowly the sounds came back again,
Now mix'd, now one by one.

Sometimes a-dropping from the sky
I heard the skylark sing;
Sometimes all little birds that are,
How they seem'd to fill the sea and air
With their sweet jargoning!

And now 'twas like all instruments,
Now like a lonely flute;
And now it is an angel's song,
That makes the Heavens be mute.

It is perhaps unnecessary to add that the comparison is between this passage and Blake's design, in the *Illustrations of the Book of Job*, of "When the Morning Stars sang together". Both the poem and the picture are at the climax of a drama of spiritual horror. Job and the Ancient Mariner have both been down into the pit to emerge at last to a scene of heavenly glory. There is both a superficial pictorial resemblance and a deeper spiritual assonance which makes it seem certain that Blake and Coleridge in their different mediums were sharing an imaginative experience (Plate 27, from the water-colour drawing done for Butts).

I cannot omit all mention of another very different member of Lamb's circle, the painter of historical pictures, Benjamin Robert Haydon. He was in many ways a man after Blake's heart, for he held strong views about the low state of art in England at that period and had great plans for its reform, plans which had no relation to the Royal Academy and the Old Gang established at its head. Like Blake, Haydon lived only for art, though his ambitions were more grandiose. Both Blake and Haydon were intimate friends of Fuseli the Swiss painter, and through this link alone it seems quite certain that they must have met before the

year 1811 when Fuseli died. Yet all through Haydon's voluminous journals, table-talk, and letters, there is no mention of
Blake whatever, so that an important potential source of information about Blake is silent. Gilchrist in his *Life of Blake* tells one
anecdote which may perhaps have been retailed by Haydon,
though the name is not given:[1] "A historical painter of the class
endlessly industrious yet for ever unknown, was one day pointing out to a visitor some favourite specimen of hopeless hugeness,
and said, 'Mr. Blake once paid me a high compliment on that
picture. It was on the last occasion when the old gentleman
visited me, and his words were, "Ah! that is what I have been
trying to do all my life—to paint *round* and never could!"'
This may be taken as an instance of the courteous care with
which Blake would find some agreeable word for an inoffensive
inferior in art." Through Haydon Blake might have met Keats
. . . but conjecture of this kind will lead me from my proper
theme, and the temptation must be resisted.

Two other friends of Lamb, who were also acquaintances of
Blake, were Thomas Griffiths Wainewright, painter, critic,
journalist, and, later, criminal, and H. F. Cary, translator of
Dante. Little record remains of their contacts with Blake,
though Gilchrist, who knew Cary in later years and evidently
gathered what information he could from him, refers to Wainewright's "intimacy with Blake, whom he assisted by buying
two or three of his expensive illustrated books". Gilchrist adds
the statement that "Blake entertained . . . a kindness for him and
his works". Certain it is that Wainewright included in an article
published in the *London Magazine* for September 1820, under
the pseudonym of Janus Weathercock, a facetious reference to
Blake's *Jerusalem*. "It contains a good deal anent one *Los*, who

[1] Mr. Edmund Blunden suggests the name of Solomon Hart as more likely.

it appears, is now, and hath been, from the creation, the *sole* and fourfold dominator of the celebrated city of Golgonooza! . . . the redemption of mankind hangs on the universal diffusion of the doctrines broached in this MS." Wainewright may not have met Blake in person until two or three years later and there is no evidence that he owned a copy of *Jerusalem*, though he certainly possessed a very fine copy of the *Songs of Innocence and of Experience* made by Blake in 1825,[1] and he subscribed for a copy of the *Illustrations of the Book of Job*.

Cary's biographer[2] thinks that it was most likely Wainewright who introduced Cary to Blake, in 1825, the year in which Crabb Robinson, calling on Blake on December 17, found him at work on the Dante illustrations with Cary's translation open before him. Gilchrist does not seem to have obtained much help from Cary, though he records that, after getting to know Blake, Cary abandoned the idea that he was mad, and simply pronounced him an "enthusiast". Immediately after Blake's death Cary bought from his widow the water-colour painting of "Oberon and Titania" now in the Tate Gallery.

It may not be fair to include William Wordsworth as a member of Lamb's circle. Wordsworth certainly numbered many of them among his friends, and was sometimes seen in Lamb's house with the others, but for the most part he remained aloof in his home in Westmorland, and there is no suggestion that he and Blake ever met one another. Crabb Robinson would have liked to see the meeting, and he did see to it that they knew and appreciated one another's poetry. As early as 1812 he read Wordsworth some of Blake's poems. He reported: "He was

---

[1] Copy P in my census (*Bibliography*, 1921). Afterwards bought by John Linnell and now the property of Mrs. Philip S. Collins of Philadelphia.

[2] R. W. King, *The Translator of Dante* (Secker, 1925), p. 170.

pleased with some of them, and considered Blake as having the elements of poetry a thousand times more than either Byron or Scott". They must often have discussed Blake on other occasions, and in 1825 and 1826 Blake was expressing to Crabb Robinson his opinions of Wordsworth. He thought Wordsworth was no Christian, but a Platonist, and asked whether he believed in the Scriptures. He had been greatly upset by a passage in the introduction to the *Excursion*, which runs as follows:

> Jehovah—with his thunder and the choir
> Of shouting angels, and the empyreal thrones—
> I pass them unalarmed.

So upset was he, indeed, that he told Crabb Robinson it had given him a bowel complaint which nearly killed him. Blake finally set down Wordsworth as a pagan, but still with great praise as the greatest poet of the age. In a letter to Dorothy Wordsworth written in February 1826, Crabb Robinson tells her, "I had the pleasure of reading to Blake in my best style the Ode on Immortality (and you know I am vain on that point and think I read Wordsworth's poems peculiarly well). I never witnessed greater delight in any listener and in general Blake loves the poems. . . ." "I doubt", he adds, "whether what I have written [about Blake] will excite your and Mr. W.'s curiosity, but there is something so delightful about the Man—tho' in great poverty with such genuine dignity and independence, scorning presents and of such native delicacy in words, that I have not scrupled promising introducing him and Mr. W. together. He expressed his thanks strongly, saying, 'You do me honour. Mr. W. is a great man. Besides he may convince me I am wrong about him. I have been wrong before now.'" The occasion for this meeting never came, and eighteen months later Blake was dead. More than twenty years later, however, Blake was again in the minds of the Wordsworth household. Edward Quillinan, Wordsworth's son-in-law, writing to Crabb Robinson from Rydal Mount in July 1848, remarks, "Among some new books that I have been looking at here this morning I observed C. Lamb's Letters and Blake's Poems—and as I was glancing over them for an hour or two, it seemed to me that both publications had the fault of *too much*. In Lamb's *too much* of childish fun, or rather that strain at fun which is the trivial imitation of child's fun; And some of Blake's verses, illustrated in the book you possess, want in this publication [evidently the Pickering edition of 1839] the poetry of the painting to support them. They seemed to sound very like nonsense-verses as we read them aloud. *Some* of them I say; for others have a real charm in their wildness and oddness. Do not suppose I undervalue the man. I have on the contrary a sort of tenderness for him that makes me disposed perhaps to overestimate the value of many of his verses. He and that good old wife of his are two very interesting persons in my mind."

In 1848 Blake was already almost completely forgotten by the world, and it is pleasant to think that he and his "good old wife" were remembered .with interest at Rydal Mount. Blake had suffered an eclipse more complete than Charles Lamb, Southey, Hazlitt, Coleridge or Wordsworth have ever done. They all thought him mad, and I touched on the queerness of his mind at the outset of my remarks. But to say that a man like Blake is mad is but a crude way of saying that he has the kind of genius which does not easily communicate its message to the generality of mankind. An attempt has been made here to give some idea of the real impression created by Blake on Lamb and his circle. The material is incomplete and the picture, I fear, has been but imperfectly painted.

X

BLAKE'S COPPER-PLATES

Blake used the metal plate for the production of a large proportion of his literary and artistic output. He had been trained as a copper-plate engraver by Basire during his boyhood, and he set up as a print producer in the style of the period shortly after his apprenticeship ended. Business in this line could not last long, however, for he was unable to remain in the ordinary rut, and once his irrepressible tendency to "originality" had taken charge he had said farewell to worldly success. From ordinary engraving he passed about 1788, when he was thirty-three, to his peculiar process of "illuminated printing", in which both the letter-press and the designs for his books were recorded on metal plates, either copper or pewter, chiefly by etching them with an acid, the text and decorations having been first written and drawn on the metal with a resistant medium.[1] The result was a form of stereotype. From 1788 until 1818 he was intermittently occupied with the etching, printing and colouring of these "illuminated books", and a total of at least 363 plates of various sizes were completed. These formed an important part of his stock-in-trade, for he was printing small numbers of all his books throughout this period. His successive removals from one part of London to another, and, in 1800, for three years to Sussex, must have been complicated by the necessity for carting several

[1] Or perhaps transferred to the plate from paper, as recent investigations by Mr. Ruthven Todd seem to shew.

hundredweights of metal in addition to his other paraphernalia and scanty household goods. The weight of metal was not, however, quite so great as it might have been, because Blake observed a certain degree of economy by using both sides of many of the plates. The ordinary engraver, if he makes a mistake, can beat up the metal in any small area from the back and then re-engrave the surface, a procedure which effectually prevents him from using the back of the plate for another engraving. Blake's etching process did not allow of his easily correcting mistakes in this way. He could erase, and this he occasionally did, but corrections of text other than very small ones had to be made by etching another plate, and this he is also known to have done in a few instances.

The proof that Blake used both sides of some of his plates is to be found in the presence of a plate-maker's mark on some of the uncoloured prints, and this was presumably stamped on one side of the plate only. This mark can be deciphered as *Jones and Pontifex, No. 47 Shoe Lane, London*, a firm represented up to recent times by Messrs. H. Pontifex and Sons, Ltd., Engineers, 43 Shoe Lane.

In addition to the etched plates, Blake made and kept a few engraved plates, such as the large one (14×38 inches) of "The Canterbury Pilgrims", which has survived to the present day and was sold with the collection of the late A. Edward Newton in New York, April 17, 1940, for $2,300.00. In the last years of his life he also engraved the twenty-one plates for his *Illustrations of the Book of Job*[1] and the seven large plates for Dante's *Inferno*. These became the property of his friend and benefactor,

---

[1] He was still dealing with the same firm when he bought the plates for the *Job* in 1823, for eighteen of them are stamped on the back *Pontifex & Co., 2 Lisle Street, Soho, London.* One has the stamp *G. Harris, No. 31 Shoe Lane, London.*

SONGS OF Innocence

1789

The Author & Printer W Blake

The Ecchoing Green

The Sun does arise,
And make happy the skies.
The merry bells ring,
To welcome the Spring
The sky-lark and thrush,
The birds of the bush,
Sing louder around,
To the bells chearful sound,
While our sports shall be seen
On the Ecchoing Green.

Old John with white hair
Does laugh away care,
Sitting under the oak,
Among the old folk,

They.

The Lamb

Little Lamb who made thee
Dost thou know who made thee
Gave thee life & bid thee feed.
By the stream & o'er the mead;
Gave thee clothing of delight,
Softest clothing wooly bright;
Gave thee such a tender voice,
Making all the vales rejoice;
Little Lamb who made thee
Dost thou know who made thee

Little Lamb I'll tell thee,
Little Lamb I'll tell thee;
He is called by thy name,
For he calls himself a Lamb:
He is meek & he is mild,
He became a little child;
I a child & thou a lamb,
We are called by his name.
Little Lamb God bless thee,
Little Lamb God bless thee.

D

Nurses Song

When the voices of children are heard on the green
And laughing is heard on the hill;
My heart is at rest within my breast
And every thing else is still

Then come home my children the sun is gone down
And the dews of night arise
Come come leave off play, and let us away
Till the morning appears in the skies

No no let us play, for it is yet day
And we cannot go to sleep
Besides in the sky the little birds fly
And the hills are all coverd with sheep

Well well go & play till the light fades away
And then go home to bed
The little ones leaped & shouted & laughd
And all the hills ecchoed

SONGS
of
EXPERIENCE

The Author & Printer W. Blake

HOLY THURSDAY

Is this a holy thing to see,
In a rich and fruitful land,
Babes reduced to misery,
Fed with cold and usurous hand?

Is that trembling cry a song?
Can it be a song of joy?
And so many children poor?
It is a land of poverty.

And their sun does never shine,
And their fields are bleak & bare,
And their ways are filld with thorns,
It is eternal winter there.

For where-eer the sun does shine,
And where-eer the rain does fall:
Babe can never hunger there,
Nor poverty the mind appall.

LONDON

I wander thro' each charter'd street
Near where the charter'd Thames does flow
And mark in every face I meet
Marks of weakness, marks of woe.

In every cry of every Man,
In every Infants cry of fear
In every voice, in every ban,
The mind-forg'd manacles I hear

How the Chimney sweepers cry
Every blackning Church appalls;
And the hapless Soldiers sigh
Runs in blood down Palace walls

But most thro' midnight streets I hear
How the youthful Harlots curse
Blasts the new born Infants tear
And blights with plagues the Marriage hearse

INFANT SORROW

My mother groand. my father wept.
Into the dangerous world I leapt:
Helpless, naked, piping loud:
Like a fiend hid in a cloud

Struggling in my fathers hands
Striving against my swadling bands,
Bound and weary I thought best
To sulk upon my mothers breast.

John Linnell, and the *Job* plates were deposited by the Linnell family trustees in the British Museum in 1918. The seven Dante plates narrowly escaped destruction, being recovered from an out-house after the death of one of the surviving trustees in 1937, and they are now in the Lessing J. Rosenwald collection, National Gallery, Washington. The etched plates for the Illuminated Books have been less fortunate, and in fact out of the large number which Blake made only one small fragment has survived. This is a piece of a copper-plate made for *America*, 1793, but afterwards re-etched in order that alterations might be made. The rejected plate was cut up by Blake, and the unused side of this piece was used by Tommy Butts, son of Blake's most faithful patron, for his own amateur efforts at engraving a head of John the Baptist under Blake's tuition. It was found in a small engraving cabinet formerly in the Butts collection, and at the sale of Lt.-Col. W. E. Moss's Blake collection at Sotheby's in 1937 was bought by Dr. Rosenbach for £50, on behalf of Mr. Lessing J. Rosenwald.

It is probable that Blake kept all the plates made for his published books up to the time of his death, and that they passed under the control of Frederick Tatham after Mrs. Blake's death in 1831. Some of them were soon afterwards taken out and printed, for copies are known of *Songs of Innocence and of Experience*, *Europe*, *America* and *Jerusalem*, all printed on Whatman paper with watermark dated 1831 or 1832. Nothing further is known of any of the plates with the exception of those for *Songs of Innocence and of Experience*. In Gilchrist's *Life of Blake*, first published in 1863, prints were included of sixteen of the *Songs*, and it is stated concerning the plates that "the gentleman from whom they were obtained had once the entire series in his possession; but all save these ten [six being etched on both sides] were stolen by an ungrateful black he had befriended, who sold them to a smith as old metal". It might be supposed that these ten plates at least might have survived until the present day, but the sad tale of loss or destruction has to be continued. Enquiries made in past years of Messrs. Macmillan, the publishers of Gilchrist's *Life*, have failed to obtain any news of the whereabouts of the original plates. In 1926 the late Laurence Binyon found, however, that electrotypes of the plates, at any rate, were still in the possession of Messrs. Clay and Son, of Bungay, who had printed Gilchrist's *Life* for Macmillan. Binyon was allowed to examine some of these, and noted that a tool had been used to scoop the hollows on the plate to a greater depth.[1] In 1942 Mr. Ruthven Todd again addressed inquiries to the printers, and by the courtesy of Messrs. Macmillan I was allowed to acquire a duplicate set of the sixteen electrotypes. The interest of these blocks is very great because, being electrotypes, they are exact reproductions of Blake's plates, so that something can be learnt from them of his technique. Careful examination of the surfaces, on two of which traces of the plate-maker's stamp are visible, shews that Blake undoubtedly first traced both the lettering and the design on the copper with the same resistant medium. The plate was then etched with acid to no very great depth, but deeply enough to allow the text to stand out as a stereotype. Blake then gouged out some of the larger spaces more deeply to prevent unwanted ink from showing in the print, and finally added more or less detail to the designs by means of the graver. Some of the plates were not touched by the graver at all, particularly among the *Songs of Experience*, where Blake seems to have aimed at a somewhat harsher effect than in the *Songs of Innocence*. On others many engraved lines were added which profoundly affected the

[1] *The Engraved Designs of William Blake* (London, 1926), p. 10.

appearance of the finished prints by helping to break up the larger flat surfaces, as in the tongues of flame twining around the text of "The Divine Image" in the *Songs of Innocence*.

A few sets of the sixteen prints were made for my own use, and the blocks were then deposited in the Fitzwilliam Museum, Cambridge; a second set of electrotypes was made in 1947, and eight of these are printed here.

XI

NEW LINES FROM "JERUSALEM"

Blake's *Jerusalem*, the last of his great epics, was begun about 1804 after he had returned to London from Felpham, where he had suffered so much from William Hayley's well-meant, though uncomprehending, patronage. The composition of the whole work and the etching of the 100 copper-plates occupied at least fourteen years, for, although the title-page is dated 1804, none of the extant copies of the book can have been printed before 1818, the earliest date which appears in the watermarks of the paper used. It is thus not possible to assign an accurate date to any one of the plates, though it is probable that they were made more or less in the order in which they stand in the completed book.

The first plate of *Jerusalem* serves as a "frontispiece", being without text in any of the five complete copies printed by Blake, which are all that have so far been described. This plate represents a figure in hat and cloak, with a fiery globe suspended from his right hand, entering a stone doorway, and has been taken to represent "Los entering the bosom of Albion". Los, in Blake's mythology, is Imagination, or the Spirit of Prophecy, and Albion is the original Man, the first inhabitant of Britain. Jerusalem, Albion's emanation or feminine counterpart, was separated from him at the Fall, and the poem *Jerusalem* recounts the story of Albion's regeneration and reunion with Jerusalem, and of his awakening, after the passage through Eternal Death, to Spiritual Freedom.

NEW LINES FROM "JERUSALEM"

Although the first plate exhibited no sort of text in the published examples of the book, I had noticed that traces of lettering could be seen on the archway and on the stones above it, though this had been very effectively obliterated. After Blake's death in 1827 the copper-plates passed with his other effects into the possession of Frederick Tatham, who printed at least three complete copies from them. These are distinguished from Blake's own prints by the watermarks, which are dated 1831 or 1832, and by the colour of the ink in which they are printed. Blake printed four of his five copies in black, and left them uncoloured; the fifth, which he coloured with great magnificence, is printed in orange.[1] Tatham, on the other hand, printed the plates in a rich red-brown. One of these posthumous copies has been for many years in the Fitzwilliam Museum, Cambridge, and I found that careful examination of the first plate enabled me to decipher most of the seven lines above the archway and some of the words on the right of the archway itself. Those on the left were too indistinct for anything to be made out. These fragmentary lines I printed in the notes to the three-volume edition of Blake's *Writings* (Nonesuch Press, 1925, vol. iii, p. 409), but I have not hitherto thought it expedient to incorporate them in the text.

Recently there has come into my possession an early proof of the plate (Plate 30) in which almost the whole of the lettering is made plain, so that the lines can now be added with full confidence to the canon of Blake's writings. To print this proof Blake used the blank side of a proof of the title-page of *Europe*, an earlier illuminated book dating from 1794. The *Jerusalem* plate is printed in two colours, so that the right-hand side and upper part of the archway is light brown while the figure and the left-

---

[1] A portion (the first twenty-five plates) of another similar coloured copy has recently come to light and is described on p. 116.

hand side of the archway shade off into a dense black, producing a sombre and splendid effect. The lettering, which would otherwise have been very indistinct, Blake has carefully outlined in black with a fine pen, with the exception of the first three or four words of the seventh line; these he has completely erased after the printing of the plate, leaving a narrow white space. The first word, O, is visible in the posthumous printing. Blake's original intention is now revealed in this proof, which is, as far as I know, unique and unrecorded. The text is as follows:

Above the archway:

> There is a Void outside of Existence which if entered into
> Englobes itself & becomes a Womb, such was Albions Couch
> A pleasant Shadow of Repose calld Albions lovely Land
> His Sublime & Pathos become Two Rocks fixd in the Earth
> His Reason his Spectrous Power, covers them above
> Jerusalem his Emanation is a Stone laying beneath
> O . . . behold the Vision of Albion.

On the right-hand side of the archway:

> Half Friendship is the bitterest Enmity said Los
>   As he enterd the Door of Death for Albions sake Inspired
> The long sufferings of God are not for ever there is a Judgment.

On the left-hand side of the archway, in reversed writing:

> Every Thing | has its | Vermin O Spectre of the Sleeping Dead!

The few stops included are the only ones supplied by Blake. A full discussion of the import of these lines would involve a more extensive survey of Blake's difficult mythology and occultism than can be attempted here. If taken, however, in conjunction with the rest of the book, it is clear that Blake first intended his frontispiece to convey the theme of the whole work. Later he seems to have decided that this was unnecessary, the theme being announced more briefly in the first two lines of the poem:

Of the Sleep of Ulro! and of the passage through
Eternal Death! and of the awaking to Eternal Life.

Ulro is material existence, as opposed to the life of Imagination.

Nevertheless, readers who set a value on every scrap of Blake's writing will be grateful for the additional statement of the nature of Albion's lovely Land, that is the "England's green & pleasant Land" of the well-known poem, so confusingly and erroneously called *Jerusalem*, although it is found at the beginning of his earlier work, *Milton*.

It is satisfactory, too, to possess Blake's new aphorism, "Half Friendship is the bitterest Enmity". This may be set beside the much earlier aphorism, "Opposition is True Friendship", from *The Marriage of Heaven and Hell*, 1790, and his tortured cry "To H——", that is "To Hayley", scribbled down in his notebook about 1809:

Thy Friendship oft has made my heart to ake:
Do be my Enemy for Friendship's sake.

It will be of interest to add to the description of this new discovery an account of the few copies of *Jerusalem* that are at present known. This census was first attempted in my *Bibliography of Blake*, 1921, and is now revised and brought up to date.

The watermarks in the Whatman paper used by Blake give a clear indication of how he built up the different copies. No printing was begun before 1818 or completed before 1820. No copies are known to have been printed in the years 1821–23. The last copy was completed in 1826, the year before Blake's death. In the first year, 1818, he started to make a coloured copy, but took it no further than plate 25. Two years later, in 1820, he printed a complete copy in orange, and eventually coloured the whole of it. Presumably it was this copy of which Blake wrote on April 12, 1827, to George Cumberland:

The last work I produced is a poem entitled Jerusalem, the Emanation of the Giant Albion, but find that to print it will cost my time the amount of Twenty Guineas. One I have Finish'd. It contains 100 Plates, but it is not likely I shall get a Customer for it.

Blake did not, in fact, find a customer for it, and it seems to have passed with his other effects to Frederick Tatham. It has usually been assumed, on the authority of this remark by Blake, that only one complete coloured copy of the work has ever existed, but I was informed in 1920 by the late James Tregaskis, a well-known bookseller, that another coloured copy was sold by him to John Ruskin about 1885. I then communicated with Mr. Arthur Severn, the owner of Ruskin's library, and he stated that he had a distinct recollection of there having been such a book in the collection, but that he believed Ruskin cut it up. There is, moreover, evidence mentioned in Sotheby's *Catalogue of Fourteen Illuminated Manuscripts, the property of Henry Yates Thompson*, June 22, 1921 (p. 148), that Ruskin was in the habit of cutting to pieces illuminated MSS., however valuable, that were in his possession. A collection of miscellaneous water-colour drawings, which was at one time deposited in the Print Room at the British Museum, contained some exquisitely coloured fragments evidently cut from leaves of a copy of *Jerusalem*, and these may possibly be some surviving evidence of the extraordinary act of destruction ascribed to Ruskin. Other separate leaves coloured by Blake are also to be met with. Two of these, each with a plate printed on both sides, are in the British Museum Print Room and the Victoria and Albert Museum. Three other leaves, each printed and coloured on both sides, were formerly in the Buxton Forman collection, sold at the

NEW LINES FROM "JERUSALEM"

Anderson Galleries, New York, March 15, 1920, (lot 67, $610.00) and were afterwards in the possession of Mr. Arthur F. Egner, New Jersey. An example of plate 51, representing Vala, Hyle and Scofield, was in the John Linnell collection, sold at Christie's, March 15, 1918 (lot 158, Martin, 70 guineas). This shewed stitch-holes near the left-hand margin, and it was numbered by Blake 51, but there is no evidence that this was taken from a complete coloured example of the book; more probably Blake took this leaf from an uncoloured copy, which he has been unable to sell, and coloured it as a specimen for Linnell. Another coloured example of the same plate was formerly in Mr. Graham Robertson's collection and is now in the Tate Gallery. Separate leaves of the ordinary issue in black are also sometimes seen. One such, a specially fine impression of an early state of plate 37 with a blue and grey water-colour wash over the central portion, is in my own collection. Prints from plates 9 (coloured), 19 (in blue), 20 (in black), 28 (in black with touches of red), 28 (duplicate, in green), 48 (in grey), 50 (in black), 58 (in grey), 78 (in black) were sold with the collection of George C. Smith, jr., New York, on November 2, 1938 (Parke-Bernet Galleries, lot 40); and of plate 50 (in black), 51 (in sepia), 99 (in sepia) in the same sale (lot 41).

CENSUS
Copies A, A*, B, C, D, E, F 1818–26

(A) 100 plates on 100 leaves. Watermark *J Whatman* 1818, 1819 or 1820. Printed in black. Several plates touched up with sepia and chinese white, and on plate 16 there is some green tinting; otherwise uncoloured. Foliated by Blake 1-100. Arrangement (using copies C, D and E as a standard, since they are uniform as to order): 1-28, 33-41, 43-46, 42, 29-32, 47-100. Bound in vellum. Size 32 × 25 cm.
John Linnell's copy, sold with his collection at Christie's, March 15,

NEW LINES FROM "JERUSALEM"

1918 (lot 194, Edwards, £89). Then acquired by the late Frank Rinder, and now in the possession of his widow.

Exhibited: Burlington Fine Arts Club, 1927, no. 88;
Paris, Brussells, Zürich, Tate Gallery, 1947, no. 41.

(A*) 25 plates on 25 leaves. Watermark *J Whatman* 1818 in 6 leaves. Printed in light red-brown and painted with water-colour washes. Consists of the first 25 plates, foliated by Blake 1-25. In a Roxburgh binding together with copies, hitherto unrecorded, of *America* and *Europe*. Size about 37·5 × 27 cm., the leaves untrimmed. The frontispiece faces the title-page, but stitch-holes in the free edge show that Blake had placed it the other way.

This volume was sold with the library of P. A. Hanrott at Evans's rooms, Part I, July 19, 1833 (lot 642). Inside the cover is the book-plate of Henry Cunliffe, and a fly-leaf is marked "Toovey 10-10-0", *i.e.* bought by Cunliffe from the dealer, C. J. Toovey, probably about 1850. Bequeathed by Cunliffe to his great-nephew, the present Lord Cunliffe, who kindly allowed me to make this description in December 1945.

(B) 100 plates on 100 leaves. Watermark *J Whatman* 1818, 1819, or 1820. Printed in black. Uncoloured except for occasional grey water-colour washes. Foliated by Blake 1-100. Arrangement as in copy A. Bound in half-morocco, gilt edges. Size 32·5 × 27 cm.

Now in the Print Room of the British Museum, having been purchased from Messrs. Evans in 1847.

(C) 100 plates on 100 leaves. Watermark *J Whatman* 1820. Printed in black with a single framing line round each plate. Retouched with indian ink, and here and there lightly washed with brown. Other-wise uncoloured. Foliated by Blake 1-100. Unbound. Size 33·5 × 26·5 cm.

Formerly in the collection of E. W. Hooper, and bequeathed by him to his daughter, Mrs. Thoron, Boston, Mass. In 1941 given by Mrs. Thoron to Harvard College Library in memory of her father.

Exhibited: Boston Museum, 1891, no. 8; Philadelphia Museum of Art, 1939, no. 113.

NEW LINES FROM "JERUSALEM"

A note was inserted by E. W. Hooper that this copy was used as a basis for the Pearson facsimile of 1877.

(D) 100 plates on 100 leaves. Watermark *J Whatman* 1820. Printed in orange. Magnificently coloured with water-colour washes and gold. Foliated by Blake 1-100. Bound in dark-green morocco, with clasps, together with the MSS., on 12 leaves, of Tatham's *Life of Blake*. Bound with the MS. are a pencil drawing of Mrs. Blake by George Richmond after Tatham, and drawings of Blake by Tatham at the ages of twenty-eight and sixty-nine. Size 33·5 × 27·5 cm.

Frederick Tatham's copy, to whom it passed with Blake's other effects after Mrs. Blake's death in 1832. It was sold at Christie's from an anonymous source on June 1, 1887 (lot 225, Quaritch, £166), and was bought from Quaritch about 1893 by General Archibald Stirling of Keir. Now the property of Lt.-Col. William Stirling of Keir.

Exhibited: Burlington Fine Arts Club, 1927, no. 89.

[A facsimile of this book in colour, with an introduction and commentary by Joseph Wicksteed, is now being prepared for publication in London.]

(E) 100 plates on 100 leaves. Watermark *J Whatman* 1824 or 1826. Printed in black. Uncoloured except for grey water-colour washes on a few plates. Foliated by Blake 1-100. Bound in red straight-grained morocco by F. Bedford, with the addition of proofs of plates 28 and 45, the latter lacking the last line. Size 36·5 × 26·5 cm. Formerly in the possession of C. J. Toovey. Now in The Pierpont Morgan Library, New York.

Exhibited: Philadelphia Museum of Art, 1929, no. 14.

[(F) A copy was believed to be in the possession of Mr. Felix Isman, New York, in 1921, but was not available then for a description to be made. No further information has been obtained since.]

Copies G, H, I, Posthumous, 1831–32

(G) 100 plates on 100 leaves. Watermark *J Whatman* 1831 or 1832. Printed in red-brown. Uncoloured. Bound in contemporary morocco, elaborately tooled, gilt edges. Size 28·5 × 23 cm.

NEW LINES FROM "JERUSALEM"

Samuel Boddington's copy, with his bookplate. Sold at Sotheby's, November 1895. Afterwards in the possession of Charles Fairfax Murray, and given by him in 1912 to the Fitzwilliam Museum, Cambridge.

(H) 100 plates on 100 leaves. Watermark *J Whatman* 1831 or 1832. Printed in red-brown. Uncoloured. Some of the plates are numbered. Bound in morocco, gilt edges, by Leighton, with the Milnes crest on the front cover, Size 28·5 × 23·5 cm.

Formerly in the possession of Thomas Butts. Sold with part of the Butts collection at Sotheby's, March 26, 1852 (R. Monkton Milnes, £10 : 15s.). In the collection of the Earl of Crewe until March 1903, when it was again sold at Sotheby's (lot 15, Quaritch, £83). It then passed into the collection of W. A. White, New York. Now in the Lessing J. Rosenwald collection, National Gallery, Washington.

Exhibited: Grolier Club, 1905, no. 32; Philadelphia Museum of Art, 1939, no. 115.

(I) 100 Plates on 100 leaves. Watermark *J Whatman* 1831 in 24 leaves. Printed in red-brown. Uncoloured. Untrimmed, size 30·25 × 24·25 cm. Bound in contemporary half-russia. Lacks plate 16, and plate 20 is in duplicate.

Offered for sale by Sawyer, London, in June 1928. Afterwards in the Cortlandt Bishop library, sold by the American Art Association, April 5, 1938 (lot 280, Sesler, $2,700.00). Next in the possession of Mr. Moncure Biddle, and now in the Charles J. Rosenbloom collection, Pittsburgh, Pa. There is no indication of the provenance before 1928.

XII

THE HISTORY OF THE "JOB" DESIGNS

WILLIAM BLAKE in 1821 was a lonely and disappointed man. After many years of neglect and poverty he had just moved to humble apartments consisting of two rooms on the first floor of No. 3 Fountain Court, Strand, the rest of the house being occupied by his wife's brother-in-law, Baines. His circumstances at this time were at such a low ebb that he was compelled to sell to Colnaghi's the whole collection of prints which he had been forming since his boyhood, and soon afterwards, in 1822, to accept a donation of £25 from the Council of the Royal Academy. Even his oldest friend and patron, Thomas Butts, had seemed to grow cool towards him, and transactions between them, formerly so numerous, had become rare. The last purchase, in fact, that Butts is known to have made from Blake was the set of twenty-one water-colour drawings illustrating his version of *The Book of Job*, and this he is believed to have acquired in or about the year 1820, if not earlier.[1]

Blake's interest in the theme of Job and his misfortunes dated back at least to before the year 1790, and probably even to 1785, when he was twenty-eight years old. To about this year is assigned a pen-and-wash drawing[2] representing Job seated be-

[1] Story's *Life of Linnell*, i. 169.

[2] This drawing, about 12 × 18 inches, was sold at Sotheby's on April 29, 1862, lot 164, probably from the collection of Frederick Tatham. It was afterwards in the collection of F. T. Palgrave, Thomas Woolner and Miss Alice Carthew, by whom it was bequeathed in 1940 to the Tate Gallery.

tween his wife and his friends. It is primitive in technique, but the characters of the component figures are already there, very much as they are shewn in plate 10 of the final Job series designed thirty-five years later, Job's wife being on his right and the friends, pointing fingers of scorn, on his left (Plate 31).

On the back of this drawing Blake made a sketch of Job's wife as she is shewn in a later variation of the design, of which there are three versions. The earliest of these three is presumably the drawing, of approximately the same size as before, in indian ink, pen and wash, which was in the possession of Miss Brenda G. Warr in 1912.[1] This was elaborated by Blake into a very highly finished water-colour painting in sepia, and he made also a companion painting of "The Death of Ezekiel's Wife". Both of these are in the collection of Mr. W. Graham Robertson, by whose permission the Job subject is here reproduced (Plate 32). This drawing cannot be dated with exactitude, but it was probably done about 1786, which is also the approximate date of a large copper-plate engraving, about 14×19 inches, of the same subject. This engraving is known only in a single impression now in my collection, and it has not hitherto been described or reproduced. It is, however, a faithful copy of the sepia drawing, and is executed in the smooth and quiet style of Blake's earliest plates. A few years later, in 1793, he again took up this plate and must have rubbed down the greater part of it, keeping only the main outlines as a guide to his burin. He then re-engraved the plate and completely changed its character so that it became, in fact, startlingly different with a gleam of wildness. Both by the changed style of engraving and by the introduction of new details it has become highly dramatized, though it is also stronger and more profound.

[1] Sold at Sotheby's on December 17, 1928 (lot 138, Maggs, £115).

In the drawings Job is seated on the left in an attitude of despair with tears streaming down his cheeks. His wife, with her hands clasped over her knees, is seated on his left, and on her left are the three friends, gazing earnestly at Job. Eliphaz is pointing under his beard. Behind the figures are the trunks of five trees. In the engraving the positions are reversed. Job's wife is now on his right, and the friends on her right, and a zigzag of lightning is added in the background. A strange alteration is also introduced in the disposition of Job's legs. In the drawings his left leg is bare and the left foot slightly in advance of the right. In the engraving both legs are covered, the toes only being shown, but the right foot is now slightly in advance of the left. These details are of interest, since they suggest that even at this early date Blake was attaching some symbolical significance to "right" and "left" and therefore to the position of the hands and feet of his figures. Mr. Wicksteed suggests that to this is due the uncomfortable appearance of Job's feet and legs in the engraving. The reversal of the design involved reversal of the significance of the position of the feet, so that Blake has been led into giving the impression of crossed legs, with a left foot on a right leg and *vice versa*. However this may be, there was probably something of the sort in Blake's mind, the "right" and "left" symbolism beginning to be formulated in these designs. It was highly developed afterwards at the time of the final Job series, as was clearly demonstrated by Mr. Wicksteed in his book on *Blake's Vision of the Book of Job* published in 1910. In No. 10 of the later designs the subject of Job and his friends is further elaborated, and a profounder meaning given to the symbolism.

To a somewhat later date belongs another design of great importance in the evolution of the Job theme. This is a water-colour in Mr. Graham Robertson's collection showing Job's redemption, when he is answered by God out of the whirlwind. It provided the idea for No. 13 of the series, though quite different from it in detail. This picture was probably painted about 1800, though there seems to be no means of determining the exact date. It was not shewn at the exhibition of 1809 and it is possible it was done later even than this.

About the year 1807 Blake drew the only design ever done by him upon stone. The subject of this was interpreted by Mr. A. G. B. Russell in 1912 as "Job in Prosperity",[1] and the title was accepted by other authorities. These included Mr. Wicksteed,[2] but he has since discovered that the subject is really "Enoch", the ancestor of Noah, who, with his sons Shem and Japheth, represents, according to Blake, "Poetry, Painting, and Music, the three Powers in Man of conversing with Paradise, which the flood did not sweep away".[3] Enoch is seated on a stone seat with an open book on his knee carrying his name in Hebrew characters. Around him are the personifications of Painting, Poetry and Music, the last represented by a woman. Figures of inspiration float on either hand, those on the right carrying a tablet on which is inscribed in Hebrew letters part of the verse from Genesis v. 24, "And Enoch walked with God, and he was not: for God took him". Fruitful vines are climbing up the sides of the design, and the steps of the seat are decorated with Gothic arches, Blake's symbol of true art. Enoch himself is an ancient bearded figure, closely resembling Job, and this design almost certainly has some relation to Blake's later conception of Job and his family as seen in the lower part of the second illustration in the Job series, and of Job and his daughters as represented in the first water-colour for No. 20 of the series, and in No. 21, where

[1] *Engravings of William Blake* (1912), p. 91.
[2] *Blake's Vision of the Book of Job* (second edition, 1924), p. 205, n. 2.
[3] "A Vision of the Last Judgement", *Poetry and Prose* (ed. Keynes, 1939), p. 643.

they represent the three Arts in Job's state of restored prosperity. A recently discovered water-colour drawing[1] provides a directly connecting link between the lithograph and the second Job illustration. This has some features in common with the lithograph, but now definitely represents Job and his family instead of Enoch, and is clearly the foundation of the Job illustration, though the positions of the figures are reversed.

It has been conjectured by Mr. Wicksteed that the idea of Job in spiritual difficulties between his wife and his friends was suggested to Blake by his own troubles, first in 1785 between Catherine Blake on the one hand and his brother Robert and his friends on the other, and again in 1793 when his integrity as artist and "prophet" was threatened by the false friends who tried to dissuade him from the course he had marked out for himself. It is also suggested that the later conception of Job answered by God out of the whirlwind was the result of his own spiritual rebirth after the Felpham period as expressed in a letter to William Hayley in October 1804:

> I am really drunk with intellectual vision whenever I take a pencil or graver into my hand, even as I used to be in my youth, and as I have not been for twenty dark, but very profitable years.[2]

A few years later, after the total failure of the exhibition of his pictures in 1809, he was again cast down and he seemed to have been utterly deserted by friends and fortune. Little is known of Blake's life during the years 1810–18, but with the advent of Linnell and a circle of new friends there came a second spiritual rebirth after a period of profound misery and obscurity. Blake, like Job, had passed through the pit of suffering and come at

---

[1] Sold at Sotheby's on November 14, 1934, lot 551.
[2] *Poetry and Prose* (ed. Keynes, 1939), p. 900.

length to a new and better understanding of intellectual truths —to be symbolized as Job's state of restored prosperity. It may thus be seen how the idea of Job had been simmering in Blake's mind for over thirty years until about 1818 the story as a whole had assumed for him a profound significance in relation to his own experiences. It was natural, therefore, that he should then set about telling the story in his own way and embody it in the series of "Inventions", which were afterwards to be recognized as the supreme achievement of his life. Although there were only two of the Job designs which had actually taken shape before the full series was made, Blake used details or ideas from earlier compositions. A striking example of this is seen in No. 14 of the series, "When the Morning Stars sang together". The frieze of angels with uplifted arms had already been used at least twice in other compositions and may have been suggested to him by a print executed in Basire's shop while he was an apprentice about 1775 (see p. 44). Another example is seen in the magnificent colour print of "God Creating Adam", 1793, which foreshadows design No. 11 in the series, "Job's Evil Dreams". Many other resemblances could be found by searching through the whole body of Blake's work.

The first set of water-colours for the Job series was, as already stated, bought by Thomas Butts. There is no remaining record of the transaction, so that we do not know to what extent Blake profited. The drawings remained in the possession of Butts's family until his son sold them, with a large part of the Blake collection, to Richard Monckton Milnes, first Lord Houghton. They appeared for the first and last time in the sale rooms when a large portion of his father's Blake collection was sold by the Earl of Crewe at Sotheby's on March 30, 1903. The drawings (lot 17) were sold to Sabin for £5600, and were acquired by the late J. Pierpont Morgan, in whose library in New York they still remain.

Blake was clearly proud of his achievement and hoped that the drawings might be the source of further profit. Butts accordingly allowed him to borrow them in order that he might shew them to other people in the hope of finding other customers for replica sets. Only one order was obtained, and this was given in 1821 by John Linnell.

Linnell was a rising artist and engraver when in 1818 at the age of twenty-six he first met Blake, who seems to have been brought, probably by his old friend George Cumberland, to Linnell's house in Rathbone Place.[1] Linnell and Cumberland also visited Blake in South Molton Street, and soon Blake and Linnell were collaborating over the engraving of a portrait of a Baptist minister, Mr. Upton. This plate is dated June 1, 1819, and from that time until Blake's death in 1827 Linnell remained his closest friend and supporter, sometimes supplying him with means of subsistence even when his own affairs were none too prosperous. Linnell's knowledge of Blake's necessities and his admiration for the designs having prompted him to order a duplicate set, he proceeded to trace the outlines himself on September 8 and 10, 1821,[2] Blake afterwards finishing them with water-colours. This second set remained in the possession of Linnell and his descendants until the whole of their Blake collection was sold at Christie's on March 15, 1918. The Job series (lot 149) was then bought by Sabin for £3990, and was afterwards sold in America, eighteen of the drawings being acquired by Grenville Lindall Winthrop of New York, by whom they were later presented to the Fogg Art Museum at Harvard.

[1] Story's *Life of Linnell*, i. 158.
[2] *Ibid.* p 169.

THE HISTORY OF THE "JOB" DESIGNS

After Blake had completed the drawings for Linnell, no further orders were obtained, and there the matter rested for some eighteen months. Linnell was not satisfied, however, that Blake had yet developed his conception to the full, and so followed the further suggestion of a set of engravings to be made from the water-colours. A business-like agreement was accordingly drawn up which was clearly very generous to Blake, since he was to be paid as the plates were completed in advance of any receipts from the sale of prints, so that Linnell, who was also paying for the copper-plates, was to bear the whole risk of the venture. During Blake's life no profits were realized, but Linnell in spite of this chose to give Blake an extra £50 in consideration of future sales. Blake therefore received in all £150, and while he was at work on the plates, Linnell provided for his immediate needs by a regular weekly payment of varying amounts as can be seen in the original account book in which each payment is initialed by the engraver.[1] The engravings were not ready for publication until early in 1826, though dated March 8, 1825, in the imprint of each plate.[2] This will be referred to again later. The whole sum due to Blake had been paid by the middle of the next year, and a receipt for the £150 is dated July 14, 1826. Linnell himself discounted his generosity to Blake, and in a letter to Bernard Barton, the quaker poet, he stated that "this [the £25 given by the Council of the Royal Academy at his instigation] was not enough to afford him permanent support, and it was in hopes of obtaining a profit sufficient to supply his future wants that the publication of Job was begun at my suggestion and expense; but as I had also the expectation, and have still, of

---

[1] A full account of these documents will be found in the next chapter of this book, p. 135.

[2] Except for the second plate which is dated in error March 8, 1828.

remuneration (the plates being my property), I have no claim to any notice upon that account".[1] Sufficient recompense, as will be seen, was received by Linnell's descendants to justify his faith, but there can be no question of the generosity of his motives at the time.

Of the actual process of the conversion of the water-colour designs to the engraved prints nothing has yet been said. The water-colours were of considerable size, the largest being about 30 × 23 cm., whereas the engraved designs, excluding the borders, have but half this area. Blake's first task, therefore, was to make a series of pencil sketches of the approximate size of the engravings to serve as a basis for the copper-plates. These sketches were done on sheets of a peculiar paper resembling "rice paper" and were carefully kept by Linnell, who marked them, "These are Mr. Blake's reduced Drawings & studies for the Engravings of the Book of Job done for me". They include sketches, some being touched with water-colour, for all the engraved plates, except the title-page, together with one design which was not used, and a few fragmentary studies. The drawings remained in the Linnell collection until this was sold in March 1918, when they were bought for £504 on behalf of the late T. H. Riches, who had married a granddaughter of John Linnell and had so acquired a special interest in the matter. Mrs. Riches has now deposited the drawings in the Fitzwilliam Museum, Cambridge. They are for the most part unfinished and some are merely indicated, so that it was to be presumed that some more finished series must have been made before the designs could be actually engraved. Yet no other link in the chain was known to exist until March 1928, when the discovery of another set of designs in Auckland, New Zealand, was

---

[1] Russell, *Letters of William Blake* (London, 1906), p. 228.

announced. These had belonged to an artist, Albin Martin, who had been a pupil of Linnell and had emigrated about the year 1850 to New Zealand. He was born in 1813, and therefore was but fourteen years old at the time of Blake's death. No claim is made that he knew Blake, but he was afterwards acquainted with members of Blake's circle, and there can be little doubt that he received the drawings from Linnell, although there is no documentary evidence in proof of this. The drawings, which are very carefully finished in brilliant water-colours, are of approximately the same size as the engravings, and are without the decorative borders. There are a sufficient number of variations to shew that they cannot have been copied from the engravings; on the other hand they are not uniform in quality. The finest of them could not have been produced by any hand but Blake's, though it is possible that he was helped by Linnell or another in finishing those that are less good. In 1928 the drawings were the property of Martin's daughters, Miss Fanny Martin and Mrs. E. J. Hickson, who submitted them for sale at Sotheby's in December of that year. The absence of full documentary evidence of their provenance produced an atmosphere of distrust in the sale-rooms, and Mr. Gabriel Wells was allowed to secure them for £500. They were afterwards acquired by Mr. Philip Hofer for his own collection,[1] though he disposed of them a few years later to Mr. Paul Mellon.

As already related, the actual engraving of the plates occupied nearly three years, from March 25, 1823, when the agreement was signed, to early in 1826, when the plates were finally approved. They were executed wholly with the graver, and were done in the free style which Blake had recently acquired. There

[1] They were well reproduced in colour and published, with a note added by Mr. Hofer, by J. M. Dent and E. P. Dutton in 1937.

are but few other plates executed by Blake in this style, and yet the *Job* plates are done with a uniform mastery which would have been thought only to come from long practice. The minor differences between the engravings and the water-colours are numerous and have been described in the introduction to the Pierpont Morgan Library reproduction. The main difference, which is at once obvious, is in the absence of the decorative borders and texts everywhere but in the plates. The general effect of the engravings is so much enhanced by these borders that it is difficult to believe that they did not form part of the original conception in Blake's mind. Yet John Linnell, in a letter to C. W. (afterwards Sir Charles) Dilke written in 1844, has stated the opposite. He was sending Dilke a copy of the *Job*, and adds, "I have sent you a couple of proofs before the Borders as a curiosity because the Borders were an afterthought and de-signed as well as engraved upon the copper without a previous drawing".[1] The pencil sketches for the first three designs shew the tentative beginnings of the borders, but these might have been added by Blake at any stage, and none of the other draw-ings have any trace of them. A few of the early proofs of the central designs in the engravings also have some pencilled sug-gestions for the borders, but otherwise no studies for them are known to exist. It seems possible that the addition of the borders occurred to Blake as a device for making a uniform shape for each plate, since these had to embody central designs of which some were oblong and others upright. Early proofs of plates 10 and 14 are reproduced here (Plates 33 and 35).

The number of designs in the water-colour sets is twenty-one; there are twenty-four pencil sketches, but two of these are first studies and one was not used. The number of engraved plates,

[1] The original letter, as well as the two proofs, are now in my collection.

however, is twenty-two, a title-page with a design of seven angels being added to this series. The preliminary sketch for this title-page was sold for Mr. G. A. Rossetti at Sotheby's on March 27, 1929, and was bought by Mr. W. T. Spencer for £50. An inscription at the bottom has the initials of Blake's friend and biographer, Frederick Tatham, and there is a note by W. M. Rossetti on the back of the sheet.

Neither Blake nor Linnell possessed any special facilities for marketing a comparatively expensive work of art such as the *Illustrations of the Book of Job*, and it is not surprising that such amateur efforts as they made should not have succeeded in selling many copies. Presumably no copies were sent out to periodicals "for review", as no contemporary notices have been discovered. Linnell succeeded in selling some copies to his acquaintances, and it seems to have been the original intention that he should be the nominal "publisher", for proofs exist with the imprint *Published as the Act directs March 8: 1825 by J: Linnell N 6 Cirencester Place, Fitzroy Square*. The final state of the prints has, however, after the date, the words *by William Blake N⁰ 3 Fountain Court Strand*, a form which would be more in keeping with Blake's self-esteem than the earlier state. Blake himself, as references in his letters shew, endeavoured, sometimes successfully, to sell copies to friends such as Francis Chantrey, Henry Crabb Robinson and George Cumberland. Thomas Butts possessed a proof copy which was sold with his collection at Sotheby's in 1903. Cumberland did his best to dispose of copies among his acquaintances in Bristol, though with small success. Blake writing to Linnell on March 15, 1827, says, "I have receiv'd a Letter from Mr. Cumberland, in which he says he will take one Copy of Job for himself, but cannot, as yet, find a Customer for one, but hopes to do somewhat by perseverance

in his Endeavours; he tells me that it is too much Finish'd, or
over Labour'd, for his Bristol Friends, as they think".[1] In his
last letter to Cumberland himself, written on April 12, 1827,
Blake says:

I thank you for the pains you have taken with poor Job. I know too
well that the great majority of Englishmen are fond of the indefinite,
which they measure by Newton's doctrine of the fluxions of an atom,
a thing which does not exist. These are politicians, and think that
Republican art is inimical to their atom, for a line or a lineament is
not formed by chance. A line is a line in its minutest subdivisions,
straight or crooked. It is itself, not intermeasurable by anything else.
Such is Job. But since the French Revolution Englishmen are all
intermeasurable by one another: certainly a happy state of agreement,
in which I for one do not agree. God keep you and me from the divinity
of yes and no too—the yea, nay, creeping Jesus—from supposing up
and down to be the same thing, as all experimentalists must suppose.[2]

It was incumbent upon Linnell to try to reimburse himself
for the initial outlay, and for years he was offering copies to
likely buyers. In 1830 he had sent a copy "on approval" to
Bernard Barton with a letter already mentioned (p. 126), but
Barton, while expressing polite interest, pleaded poverty, and,
after trying unsuccessfully to sell a copy to someone else, added
in another letter:

There is a dryness and hardness in Blake's manner of engraving
which is very apt to be repulsive to print-collectors in general—to
any, indeed, who have not taste enough to appreciate the force and
originality of his conceptions, in spite of the manner in which he has
embodied them. I candidly own I am not surprised at this; his style
is little calculated to take with the admirers of modern engraving. It
puts me in mind of some old prints I have seen, and seems to combine

[1] *Poetry and Prose* (ed. Keynes, 1939), p. 926.
[2] *Ibid.* p. 927.

somewhat of old Albert Durer with Bolswert. I cannot but wish he could have clothed his imaginative creations in a garb more attractive to ordinary mortals, or else given simple outlines of them. The extreme beauty, elegance, and grace of several of his marginal accompaniments induce me to think that they would have pleased more generally in that state. But his was not a mind to dictate to; and what he has done is quite enough to stamp him as a genius of the highest order.[1]

Eight years later Linnell sent Barton an ordinary copy as a present, saying:

There were some reasons at the time of publication why no copies were given, but yours should have been an exception. . . . As you value the work for the invention and execution the copy sent will be to you as good as any, though I should have sent you the proof had I any number, but I have only a few copies left for there were not many printed. The price has been lowered (as you will perceive by the mark outside the cover) to the present scale of prices and is put on the label that you may not give an incorrect answer to any inquiries upon the subject.[2]

As to the actual date of publication and the price of the prints some misapprehension has arisen. Many of the existing sets have on the outer cover a printed label dated March 1826. Gilchrist stated[3] that this was the actual date of publication and not March 8, 1825, which was merely the date by which Blake had expected to finish them. That they were not completed by March 1825 is evident from a reference in a letter from Blake to Linnell dated November 10, 1825: "I have, I believe, done nearly all that we agreed on &c. If you should put on your considering Cap, just as you did last time we met, I have no doubt

[1] Story's *Life of Linnell*, i. 176-77.
[2] Letter in possession of Messrs. Tregaskis, 1932.
[3] *Life*, 1880, i. 335.

that the Plates would be all the better for it. . . . I hope a few
more days will bring us to a conclusion."[1] Probably the plates
were completed not long after this, for in February 1826 Blake
asks Linnell for "a copy of Job to shew to Mr. Chantrey" as if
the book was already finished and on sale.

As to the price at which the prints were sold, Gilchrist states
that the price of ordinary prints was 3 guineas, of proofs, 5, and
of In lia-paper proofs, 6.[2] The late E. J. Ellis stated, apparently
on the authority of John Linnell, jr., that "the proofs were published at £10:10s. the set, and the prints at £5:5s. the set,
bound in cardboard covers of terra-cotta colour with white labels
pasted in the middle upon which the price is written in pencil".[3]
That this is erroneous is shewn by some existing copies of the
prints which are bound in limp boards of a drab colour with the
price for prints and proofs marked on the cover as stated by
Gilchrist. Ellis's statement probably refers to a later binding,
Linnell or his family having continued to sell copies in small
numbers almost up to the time of the final sale of the Linnell
collection in 1918. The original price is further established by
Blake's own statement with regard to Crabb Robinson's copies.
On March 31, 1826, he wrote to Linnell, "Mr. Robinson certainly did subscribe for Prints only & not for Proofs, for I remember that he offer'd to pay me Three Guineas for each of the
Copies".[4] In 1830, when Linnell was writing the letter to
Bernard Barton already quoted, he says, "P.S. I have sent a
plain copy of the Job for your inspection. The price to you will
be the same as the trade price—£2:12:6d." which indicates
a retail price of 3 guineas. These statements have now been

[1] *Poetry and Prose* (ed. Keynes, 1939), p. 918.
[2] *Life*, 1880, i. 335.
[3] Ellis, *The Real Blake* (London, 1907), p. 409.
[4] *Poetry and Prose* (ed. Keynes, 1939), p. 920.

corroborated by the evidence of the account book described in the next chapter.

The paper upon which the engravings were printed shews some variation, but nearly all the India-paper proofs were on Whatman's Turkey Mill dated 1825. The ordinary proofs and the print state were on Turkey Mill 1825, ordinary Whatman paper, 1825, or on paper without a watermark. One complete set of India-paper proofs seems to have been finely coloured by Blake himself,[1] and four proofs also coloured by Blake are now in the Fitzwilliam Museum, Cambridge.

According to the account book (see p. 142) the initial printing was of 150 sets of proofs on India paper, 50 sets on French paper and 100 sets on drawing (i.e. Whatman) paper. How many more sets were printed in later years it is impossible to say, though it may be that no more were done. It was not generally known that the prints were obtainable and the demand was certainly very small. At the Linnell sale in 1918 presumably the whole remaining stock was sold, and this consisted of 6 bound sets of India-paper proofs (£226:16:0), 12 sets of India-paper proofs unbound (£144:18:0) and 50 sets in "print state" unbound (£346:10:0). Blake had now repaid his debt with interest.

The copper-plates, being regarded by the Linnell Trustees as a national possession, were not sold with the remainder of the collection, but were instead deposited in the Print Room of the British Museum.

---

[1] This was at one time in Sir F. Burton's collection, and was offered for sale by the bookseller, Tregaskis, in 1901. It was probably the same copy that was sold by the American Art Association, New York, April 16, 1923 (lot 118, $3,125.00); then acquired by George C. Smith and sold with his collection at the Parke-Bernet Galleries, New York, November 2, 1938 (lot 58, Sessler, $3,200.00). Another coloured copy exists, but has no provenance.

XIII

THE BLAKE-LINNELL DOCUMENTS

THE STORY of William Blake's association with the painter
John Linnell from 1818 until Blake's death in 1827 is well
known, having been first described in Gilchrist's *Life of Blake*,
1863, and supplemented in A. T. Story's *Life of Linnell*, 1892.
To Linnell Blake owed a great change in his fortunes, so that
during his last years he did not lack friends or money, while a
considerable degree of recognition was accorded to his talents.
In particular the world owes to Linnell's encouragement of his
friend, as described in the preceding chapter, one of the greatest
works of individual genius ever produced in this country, Blake's
Illustrations of the Book of Job, which culminated in the series of
twenty-one engravings published in March 1826. In 1935 the
Pierpont Morgan Library published in New York an exhaustive
study of Blake's *Job*, with reproductions of all the drawings,
water-colours and engravings, and an introduction by Laurence
Binyon and myself. Here was gathered all the information that
was then available, though for documentation of the transaction
we had to depend on the rather meagre particulars given in
Story's *Life of Linnell*.

Three years later, when Blake's wood-blocks made for
Thornton's *Virgil* so unexpectedly came to light, some interesting documents were also discovered which threw fresh light on
the genesis and publication of the *Job* engravings. These documents formed lot 62 in the sale at Christie's on December 2,

1938, when the wood-blocks were acquired for the nation. The documents were bought for 75 guineas by Messrs. Robinson on behalf of Mr. Otis T. Bradley, of New York, who has recently presented them to Yale University Library, New Haven, Conn. Although I was the first to see these documents after their discovery in the vaults of a bank, I did not have the opportunity of fully examining them either then or at the time of the sale, but photostats of them all have been sent to me by Mr. Chauncey Brewster Tinker, and by his courtesy and the permission of the Librarian of Yale University I was enabled to make them public in January 1943.[1]

According to Christie's sale catalogue the documents consisted of *William Blake's Account Book of the Subscribers and Purchasers of the Book of Illustrations of the History of Job . . .; A Memorandum of Agreement . . . between William Blake and John Linnell . . . three loose pages of an Account Book . . ., and Eleven Receipts for Money from John Linnell, signed by William Blake, of various dates.* These can now be examined in their chronological order. The earliest is a receipt from Blake dated August 12, 1818, for £2 for an unspecified object. The next three, dated from September 19 to December 31, 1818, are in Blake's hand and refer to the first commission given by Linnell to Blake —namely, the "laying-in" of an engraving after Linnell's portrait of Mr. Upton, a Baptist minister. For this plate, published June 1, 1819, Blake received in all 15 guineas, paid in several instalments. On August 27, 1819, Blake received from Linnell £1:19:6 for a copy of the *Songs of Innocence and of Experience.* Linnell gave this book to his son William in 1863, and it is now

---

[1] Another account of the documents with a fuller transcription was published by Mr. Edwin Wolf, 2nd, in vol. xxxvii of the papers of the Bibliographical Society of America, First Quarter, 1943.

in the possession of his granddaughter, Mrs. T. H. Riches, by
whom it has been deposited in the Fitzwilliam Museum, Cambridge (Keynes, copy K). On December 30 of the same year
Blake received 14 shillings for some plates of *Jerusalem, chap. 2.*
Probably this was part of the Linnell copy of *Jerusalem*
(Keynes, copy A) which now belongs to Mrs. Frank Rinder.
On April 20, 1821, he received 2 guineas for *Heaven and Hell*,
that is *The Marriage of Heaven and Hell*, first printed in 1790,
of which this is the most beautiful copy in existence (Keynes,
copy I). It was sold at Christie's with the Linnell-Blake collection in 1918 (lot 195, £756), and is now with the T. H. Riches
collection in the Fitzwilliam Museum, Cambridge. Another
receipt dated March 1, 1822, is for "Three Pounds on Acco!".
Mr. Edwin Wolf suggests that this was payment for the Linnell
copies of *America* and *Europe* (Keynes, copies N and I) which
are also now in the T. H. Riches collection.

Next in order comes the most interesting document of the
collection, the original agreement between Blake and Linnell for
the *Job* engravings. A. T. Story gave an abbreviated version
of the agreement, apparently quoting from memory (*Life of
Linnell*, i, 169). The document is written in Linnell's hand, and
is signed by both parties. It runs as follows:

Memorandum of Agreement
between William Blake and
John Linnell

March 25th, 1823.

　　　W. Blake agrees to Engrave the | set of Plates from his own
designs of | Job's Captivity in number twenty, for | John Linnell—
and John Linnell | agrees to pay William Blake five Pounds | per
Plate or one hundred Pounds for | the set part before and the remainder |
when the Plates are finished, as Mr. Blake | may require it, besides

Memorandum of Agreement
between William Blake and
John Linnell.
March 25.th 1823 —

W. Blake agrees to Engrave The
Set of Plates from his own designs of
Job's Captivity in number twenty, for
John Linnell — and John Linnell
agrees to pay William Blake five Pounds
pr. Plate or one hundred Pounds for
The Set part before and the remainder
when the Plates are finished as Mr Blake
may require it besides which J. Linnell
agrees to give W. Blake one hundred
pounds more out of the Profits of
The work as the receipts will admit of
it. signed J. Linnell Wm Blake
N. B. J. L. to find Copper Plates.

THE BLAKE-LINNELL DOCUMENTS

which J. Linnell | agrees to give W. Blake one hundred | pounds more out of the Profits of | the work as the receipts will admit of | it.

Signed   J. Linnell   Willm Blake.

N.B.   J. L. to find copper Plates.

This agreement is written on a folded sheet of paper about $6\frac{1}{2} \times 4$ inches, and on the other side is Blake's first receipt, initialed by him:

1823 March 25th
Cash on acct of Plates in the
foregoing agreement £5–5–0 W.B.

In Christie's sale catalogue already quoted, the documents are stated to include *William Blake's Account Book . . .* and *three loose pages of an Account Book.* This statement is not accurate, all the accounts referred to having been kept by Linnell. On the *three loose pages* are recorded a long series of payments made to Blake from March 1823 to October 1825, but the entries are all in Linnell's hand, each sum being initialed by Blake as he received it. On two occasions the payment was made in the form of coals, one chaldron being reckoned at £1:17s. Some of the payments had been received by Blake from subscribers to the work, including those from Flaxman and Calvert. The majority were made by Linnell in cash as required, the amounts varying from £1 to £10 at a time. From these accounts it appears that Blake received in all £150:19:3, and a separate document in Blake's hand gives a final receipt for the copyright as follows:

London July 14: 1826

Recievd of Mr John Linnell, the Sum of One | Hundred & fifty Pounds for the Copy-right & Plates | (Twenty-two in number) of the

139

London July 14: 1826

Recievd of Mr John Linnell, the Sum of One
Hundred & Fifty Pounds for the Copy-right & Plates
(Twenty-two in number) of the Book of Job. Published
by Me. William Blake Author of the Work

March 1823

Witness: Edwd Jno Chance

No 3 Fountain Court Strand)

THE BLAKE-LINNELL DOCUMENTS

Book of Job, Publishd | March 1825 by Me, William Blake Author of the Work

N° 3 Fountain Court Strand

Witness: Edwd Jno Chance

The witness, Edward John Chance, was a print dealer working at 28 London St., Fitzroy Square, as appears from an inscription in a copy of the Dante engravings formerly in the possession of the Marquess of Crewe (sold at Sotheby's, April 21, 1943, lot 312).

Blake had therefore received £150 before the question of any profits had arisen, and with this he was evidently content, though he had engraved two more plates than were originally agreed upon. Linnell had undoubtedly treated him with generosity, the degree of this generosity being now for the first time made clear. The account book already referred to was wholly Linnell's record, and consists mainly of a list of the subscribers for plain and proof sets of the engravings. The list was opened in October 1823, but the entries after this are not dated for nearly nine years, the first later date being August 1832. It is therefore not possible to say exactly how much repayment Linnell had received up to the time of Blake's death in August 1827, though it could not have been more than £142:9s. Even in 1833, when the Earl of Egremont paid 6 guineas for a proof set, the total receipts were only £167:17:6. The normal price for an ordinary set was 3 guineas, though the trade and many friends were supplied with copies at £2:12:6. The usual price for proof sets was 5 guineas, all sold to private buyers, though Mr. Butts received "1 Copy of Proofs for £3 3s. od. because he lent the Drawing to Copy". Up to and including the year 1833 only twenty-three plain sets and twenty proofs had been sold. Besides these accounts there is at the end of the book an "Account of Expenses of the Book of Job". This details the cost of copper-plates, paper, printing and binding, and is here set out in full:

1823			£	s	d
	6 copper plates for Job		1		
	6 Do	Do	1	2	
	6 Do	Do	1	3	7
1825 2	Do	Do		6	
	proofs		1		
	Do at Dixons & paper		1		
	Do at Lahee & —			10	
Sep	Proofs	& —	2		
Oct	Do	& —	2		
Nov	Binding 3 sets			7	6
			10	9	1

		£	s	d
March 1826	Paid to Mr Lahee for 150 sets of Proofs on India paper.	56	5	
	to Freeman the workman	1		
	to Mr White for Boarding	2	4	6
	1 ream of paper for Do	1	6	
	To Mr Leighton for Binding & paper &c.	13	17	
May	To Lahee for 65 setts of Job on french paper	16	3	
	To Do for 50 sets on Drawing paper	10	10	
	To Do for Do	10	10	
		£111	15	6

Linnell's total outlay, therefore, during Blake's lifetime was £262:14:9, and he remained at least £120 out of pocket at Blake's death, without any certainty of ever receiving reimbursement. In the event, Blake's repayment was more than adequate, but it was Linnell's descendants who received it (after the sale at Christie's in 1918), not the generous benefactor himself. It may be noted that Linnell paid for only twenty copper-plates, though twenty-two were engraved. This is explained by the fact that two of them (they may all be examined in the British Museum) had already been used for engraving of maps on the reverse sides and evidently were scrap metal obtained cheaply by Blake himself.

Linnell's account book need not be set out in full, many of the names appearing in it not being of special interest. Some, however, may be mentioned. The first subscriber in 1823 was Edward Hodges Baily, R.A., the sculptor, who had been a pupil of Flaxman and may have known Blake. In 1822 he had been the mover of a proposal to give Blake a grant of £25 from the Council of the Royal Academy. Among those who followed were Flaxman, Butts, Henry Crabb Robinson (three copies), C. H. Tatham, Calvert, Sir Henry Torrens, Charles Aders, T. G. Wainwright, Sir Thomas Lawrence and Bishop Jebb. Next to Sir T. Lawrence's name is the following entry: "The King—1 copy of Proofs sent by the order of Sir W^m. Knighton & Dr. Gooch, & for which 10 gns. was ordered to be paid—& was p^d by Messrs Budd & Calkin, Pall Mall".

Immediately after this is the less august entry: "Josiah Taylor Esq 1 copy of Proofs sent to the House of Correction by F. Tatham, Taylor being s^d H. of C. for swindling". The King's copy is not now to be found in the Royal Library at Windsor, though the date and occasion of its loss are not recorded.

The "Account of Expenses" provides the elucidation of a name which has hitherto puzzled Blake's biographers, that of Lahee, the copper-plate printer. In an undated letter, now to be referred to 1825, Blake makes an appointment to meet Linnell at

Lahee's house, but the name had not before been properly de-ciphered. It is also of interest to know that the original printing consisted of 150 sets of proofs on India paper, and 165 sets of ordinary prints—65 on French paper, and 100 on drawing paper. Examination of existing sets shews that the "French paper" is unwatermarked, and that the "drawing paper" is Whatman's, dated 1825. These prints remained on sale to friends of the Linnell family for almost a century after Blake's death.

Further items recorded in the account book are as follows:

1. Four payments made from August 18, 1824, to January 28, 1825, totalling £20, for "the Portrait of Mr. Lowery", an engraving of Wilson Lowry, F.R.S., engraver and inventor, with which Blake had helped Linnell.

2. A payment of £5 in 1825 "for sketches of subjects from Dante", the beginning of another great enterprise, which is not further documented here.

3. Two payments of £5 each made in October and November 1825, "on acc^t of Drawings of Paradise regained", that is, the exquisite set of twelve water-colour drawings sold in 1918 for £2205, and now in T. H. Riches collection in the Fitz-william Museum, Cambridge.

Another document is a receipt for 5 guineas received from Mrs. Aders through Linnell for a copy of *Songs of Innocence and of Experience* (Keynes, copy R), which Linnell afterwards bought back for himself and gave to his son James in 1863. It was sold at Christie's in 1918 (lot 215, £735), and is now with the T. H. Riches collection in the Fitzwilliam Museum, Cambridge. The final document is a receipt for £1:11:6, dated May 16, 1829, and signed by Frederick Tatham on behalf of Mrs. Blake for *Homers Illiad & Oddisey*. Probably this was Blake's copy of Chapman's *Homer*, folio, 1606, which A. T. Story (*Life of*

THE BLAKE-LINNELL DOCUMENTS

Linnell, i. 78) states was bought by Linnell after Blake's death.

It is obvious that these documents form only an incomplete record, not accounting for a great number of Blake's productions which were in the Linnell collection. They provide, however, interesting sidelights on Blake's relations with Linnell and add materially to our knowledge of the details of the last years of his life.

XIV

BLAKE'S "JOB" ON THE STAGE

SOME OF THE STORY of Blake's *Illustrations of the Book of Job* has been told in the two preceding chapters. The present chapter seeks to give only an idea of the meaning that Blake tried to convey by his pictures, and the history of an attempt made in recent years to convey some of this meaning to a wider audience through the media of music, dance and mime.

Blake had certainly read the Book of Job in the Bible attentively, but he chose to put a somewhat different interpretation on the story, and to make it an entirely spiritual and symbolical history of a man's mind under the blows of adversity with some important divergences from the Bible version.

The designs until comparatively recent years were taken to be illustrations of the Bible story of Job, and this was, indeed, what Blake called them—"Illustrations of the Book of Job". It was not until 1910, when Mr. J. H. Wicksteed first published his book, *Blake's Vision of the Book of Job*, that it began to be realized that the designs embodied a personal version of the Bible story, with a wealth of private symbolism and hidden meaning. This revision of the former view of Blake's pictures does not in any way detract from the full aesthetic enjoyment of their merits as pictures. On the other hand, it adds to their interest and to the appreciation of the details of their beauty, while affording some sort of explanation of why they seem so pregnant with meaning, even when the mind is not yet instructed enough to be able to

take in all that they convey. Mr. Wicksteed's work has now fully
established the importance of these designs in the development
of Blake's philosophy and art, and has demonstrated that they
may be interpreted as an account of his own misfortunes and
spiritual rebirth.

The first important clue to the understanding of the designs
is the fact that Job and Jehovah are usually represented as almost
identical figures, that is to say Blake's Jehovah is really an aspect
of Job himself, and that Satan too is a spiritual "state" of the
man. The story of the designs is then seen to be a primarily
subjective experience, "the account of a man's inward struggle
and triumph, the conflict between his indwelling Good and Evil
powers".

The argument of the spiritual drama of Job as seen by Blake
may be briefly summarized as follows. The story in the Bible is
that of a human being who regards himself as virtuous, who is
afflicted, as he believes, unjustly, and is accused, by his friends,
of sin, since there can be no reason for affliction except sin. He
denies that his misfortunes are his desert, and finally, in the Bible,
repents, not of disobeying God's laws, but of presumption in
trying to understand his ways, so that the mystery of suffering
is left unsolved. Elihu, in the Bible, is thought to be a later inter-
polation in the original story, and his speeches develop and
emphasize the words of Job's friends.

To Blake also Job is in the wrong, but his sin is one of ideas,
not action, and, unlike the Bible, Blake makes clear what he believes Job's sin to be. In this respect he diverges entirely from the
Bible, for to him Job's spiritual sin is one of materialism and
complacency. Blake's God is Divine Humanity (which he sometimes identifies as the Poetic Genius) and his Satan is constituted
by the false values in man's life, which may make mortal error

even of his goodness, an apparent paradox typical of Blake's thought. Job, therefore, living in material prosperity, protesting his own virtue, deriving false merit from his burnt-offerings and charity, is living in darkness, symbolized by the *setting* sun which illumines the first scene in the series. Satan's attacks are spiritual, though symbolized as material, and Job's self-righteousness makes him an easy prey. Job's friends, or "comforters", are false friends who exhibit to him his own failings in themselves, and when in his exasperation he at last appeals to his God, it is a vision of Satan that appears.

In Blake's story it is Elihu that brings about the turning-point in Job's spiritual history. Job has descended into the pit of suffering, deluded by his materialism and self-regard into believing himself an ill-used man. Elihu shews him the falsity of his ideals and that in crediting himself with loving others he really only loves himself. But he gives Job fresh hope even though he be old, pointing to the stars and providing by contrast the stimulus of his own youth and beauty. Job is thus brought to realize his own place in the larger scheme of things and the true nature of love. Immediately his Spiritual Self, now again the person of Jehovah, is revealed to him, and, in the designs, speaks to him out of the whirlwind. Blake then shews the regenerated character of Job in a series of visions, in one of which Satan is cast out. Job is finally reunited with Jehovah in a scene of symbolic worship, and he is restored to prosperity in this new humility, love and understanding of art—which is, to Blake, religion. He is seen at the end again with his sons and daughters in the *sunrise* of a fresh spiritual existence.

Below a pencil sketch of the supreme design of "When the Morning Stars sang together" Blake has put a "symbolic" signature—the words *done by* followed by a series of symbols (1) a straight line, the simplest figure with natural limit, *i.e.* immortality; (2) a hand; (3) a B, *i.e.* Blake; (4) an eye; (5) a circle, *i.e.* symmetry. This indicates Blake's belief that this drawing, the climax of a supreme effort, was created by the Poetic Genius in his own person. It was about 1794 that Blake had written in his poem "The Tyger" the lines:

> What immortal hand or eye
> Dare frame thy fearful symmetry?

Twenty-five years later it was his own mortal hand and eye that dared the impossible—and succeeded. The inspired symmetry of this design and of the whole *Job* series could only have been carried through by the breath of God, that is, of the Poetic Genius, or Imagination (Plates 34 and 35).

     .   .   .   .   .

The foregoing is a brief account of the idea embodied in Blake's great spiritual drama as portrayed in his series of engravings. At first sight these designs, with their rather obscure message, impress the mind with their elaborate grandeur and suggest that it would be almost impossible to adapt them for the purposes of the stage. There are several designs, such as "Behemoth and Leviathan", and "God speaking out of a whirlwind", which clearly transcend the physical limitations of any such attempt. Yet long familiarity with the designs convinced me that the inner thread of Blake's drama possessed a fundamental simplicity—and that if this could be successfully extracted it would provide the theme for a ballet of a kind which would be new to the English stage. Blake had, moreover, unconsciously provided in his pictures several settings which could easily be adapted for stage scenes, and innumerable suggestions in his figures for attitudes and groupings which cried out for their conversion by a choreographer into actuality and movement.

To be fully successful a ballet must synthesize the different arts of drama, design and colour, music and dancing. Blake had provided in his *Vision of the Book of Job*, as we may now call it, ample material to form a basis for all of these except the music. The first necessity was to fashion the "story" as a framework which could afterwards be clothed by the contributions of the various arts, and upon this initial simplification the success of the further developments would depend. It was soon evident that, after physical impossibilities had been eliminated, a spiritual drama could be evolved which would provide enough continuity of theme and variety of incident to sustain the interest of an audience for as long as a ballet of this kind could reasonably be made to last, that is to say for thirty or forty minutes. The co-operation of an artist, Mrs. Gwendolen Raverat, was obtained, and, after many months of preliminary thought and conversations, we contrived a scenario which has, with only minor alterations, formed the acting version of the ballet. The synopsis printed on the programme at all performances is as follows:

Scene 1. Job is sitting in the sunset of prosperity with his wife, surrounded by his seven sons and three daughters. They all join in a pastoral dance. When they have dispersed, leaving Job and his wife alone, Satan enters unperceived. He appeals to Heaven which opens, revealing the Godhead (Job's Spiritual Self) enthroned within. On the steps are the Heavenly Hosts. Job's Spiritual Self consents that his mortal nature be tested in the furnace of temptation.

Scene 2. Satan, after a triumphal dance, usurps the throne.

Scene 3. Job's sons and daughters are feasting and dancing when Satan appears and destroys them.

Scene 4. Job's peaceful sleep is disturbed by terrifying visions of War, Pestilence and Famine.

Scene 5. Messengers come to Job with tidings of the destruction of all his possessions and the death of his sons and daughters. Satan introduces Job's comforters, three wily hypocrites. Their dance at first simulates compassion, but this gradually changes to rebuke and anger. Job rebels, "Let the day perish wherein I was born". He invokes his vision of the Godhead, but the opening Heaven reveals Satan upon the throne. Job and his friends shrink in terror.

Scene 6. There enters Elihu who is young and beautiful. "Ye are old and I am very young." Job perceives his sin. The Heavens open revealing Job's Spiritual Self again enthroned.

Scene 7. Satan again appeals to Job's Godhead, claiming the victory, but is repelled and driven down by the Sons of the Morning. Job's household build an altar and worship with musical instruments, while the heavenly dance continues.

Scene 8. Job sits a humbled man in the sunrise of restored prosperity, surrounded by his family, upon whom he bestows his blessing.

.   .   .   .   .

It is plain that this synopsis is too much simplified to make a fully satisfying presentment of Blake's theme. Yet it contains the essential characters and situations of Blake's vision. The symmetry, already mentioned as a feature of Blake's designs and in particular of the *Job* series, is preserved. Job sits at the beginning in the sunset of material prosperity, he is tried and tormented and descends into the pit of affliction, the truth is revealed to him, and he repents, and he is seen at the end in the sunrise of a new and different prosperity. A dramatic climax is provided in the middle of the ballet when Job summons his vision of the Godhead, and Satan, to his horror, is revealed upon the throne. An effective contrast is made between the static characters of Job and his Spiritual Self, and the volcanic exuberance of Satan, Job's material and physical counterpart; another contrast is made between the double-faced contortions of the Comforters, the purity of the young and beautiful Elihu, and a broader one between the dark horror of Satan's enthronement and the severe beauty of the scene when the Godhead is restored to his place by Job's spiritual enlightenment. A variety in the stage effects is also introduced by the use of two levels, Jehovah's throne being set on a platform with a series of steps. The earthly characters move only on the stage level, while movements can be carried out by the heavenly beings around the throne and on the steps.

It was at first feared that a difficulty might arise by introducing a representation of the Deity on the stage, even though all reference to "God" in the scenario was carefully avoided. It was ascertained, however, that the Lord Chamberlain's licence did not have to be obtained as no words were used in the performance. The only risk was that of prosecution by the police under the Blasphemy Laws. It was decided that this was a risk that might justifiably be taken, though additional safety was invoked by providing Jehovah with a mask so as to make the presentation quite impersonal. This mask, rather more than life-size, was originally made by Hedley Briggs after a large drawing by Blake of the Head of Job, which is in my Blake collection.

One of the scenes which it was impossible to represent exactly on the stage was Blake's design of Job tormented on his couch by evil dreams. The liberty was, therefore, taken of representing Job's torment by a dance of Satan and his "Trinity of Accusers", called, for the purposes of the programme, "War, Pestilence, and Famine". The grouping of their exit was modelled exactly on Blake's engraving of this subject made in 1783, and they wore masks by Hedley Briggs suggesting these figures. These masks were afterwards re-designed so as to appear rather more horrific. It should be noticed that Satan during this dance reproduces the positions shewn in one of Blake's best known designs of "Satan smiting Job with boils".

The first trials of these settings were arranged on a model stage, the back scenes and the figures for the various groupings being made by Mrs. Raverat. This point in the development of the ballet was reached in 1927. In that year there were few English composers at work who had much experience of ballet music, or whose range could compass any affinity with the mind and genius of Blake. It was eventually decided to approach Dr. Ralph Vaughan Williams, O.M., and he was immediately fired with an enthusiasm for the task—though he stipulated that there should be no dancing on points, which he greatly disliked, and that the performance should not be called a "ballet". The prospect of getting the piece performed on the stage was then felt to be less remote than before, and plans were laid for introducing the idea to Serge Diaghileff, who was then visiting London with the Ballets Russes de Monte Carlo. A French version of the scenario was prepared and was put before Diaghileff together with a book of full-sized reproductions of the engravings. But this proved abortive, the projected ballet being pronounced to be "too English", and "too old-fashioned"—although it was, in fact, an entirely new conception of the possibilities of representation of a spiritual theme by means of dancing. The book of engravings was, however, not returned, and it was interesting to see distinct traces of Blake's influence appearing in another Biblical ballet "The Prodigal Son", produced by Diaghileff in his following London season.

It now seemed unlikely that the ballet would be performed, and Dr. Vaughan Williams completed his music on the assumption that it would be played rather as a concert piece, orchestrating it for some eighty instruments. It was finished early in 1930, and was performed for the first time by the Queen's Hall Orchestra at the Thirty-third Norfolk and Norwich Triennial

Musical Festival on October 23, being conducted by the composer. It is interesting, in view of subsequent events, to record the impression received at this first performance by the musical critic of *The Times*, who wrote: "The work suffered from being stage music without the stage. Vaughan Williams's Pageant for Dancing is founded on Blake's illustrations of the Book of Job, and planned in nine scenes, with an epilogue. A concert version of such a work can be little more satisfactory than is the orchestral accompaniment to a song-cycle without the singer. All that can be said is that the hearing of the music makes one want to have a realisation of the ballet worthy alike of Blake and Vaughan Williams. The music, in its acceptance of form and its rejection of formalism, is of a piece with Blake. It contained tunes of such simple beauty that one seems to have known them always, but their lines lead on into a realm of musical thought that one enters for the first time. The 'Saraband of the Sons of God', Job's dream, and the Pavan and Galliard of 'the ultimate vision', the last two worked together into the long epilogue, are salient instances."

The music, in fact, met with general approval, and it was played a second time when it was broadcast from the London Regional Station on Savoy Hill on February 13, 1931.

Before this date the settings on the model stage had been shown to Dame Lilian Baylis and Miss Ninette de Valois, and had won their approval. Plans were, indeed, going actively forward for a production of the ballet (to be called, in deference to the composer's wishes, a "masque for dancing") at the fourth season of the Camargo Society, which had been formed in 1930 to foster the art of ballet in England, lest after the death of Diaghileff it should fall into decay. I made myself responsible for the initial expenses, being generously assisted by Dr. J. N.

BLAKE'S "JOB" ON THE STAGE

Keynes and Sir Thomas Dunhill, and I provided Miss de Valois with all the available reproductions of the whole range of Blake's designs. She made a close study of these, taking from them many suggestions of attitude and gesture, and this helped to sustain the Blakean atmosphere throughout the ballet. The scenery and costumes were made after Mrs. Raverat's designs, and the concert music was rescored for a much smaller orchestra by Mr. Constant Lambert. The first performances of the ballet were given at the Cambridge Theatre in London on July 5 and 6, 1931. The part of Satan was created by Mr. Anton Dolin, and that of Elihu by Mr. Stanley Judson. The ballet was repeated three weeks later by the same company during the Ninth Annual Festival of the International Society for Contemporary Music at Oxford.

Blake's *Vision of the Book of Job* was fully established in its stage form by these three performances, and it was greeted by *The Times* critic as "a completely satisfying synthesis of the arts". A month after the performance at Oxford an independent version of the ballet was given at the Lewisohn Stadium in New York, and in September 1931 the original version was incorporated in the repertory of the Vic-Wells Ballet under the direction of Miss Ninette de Valois. It was revived by the Camargo Society during a four weeks' season in June and July 1932, and was given by the same company in Copenhagen on September 25. It was for this revival that I made the addition of the drop-scene showing Blake's celebrated design of "God creating the Universe", which may serve to attune the audience to the power of Blake's mind before the ballet begins, though its suitability has been criticized on other grounds.

Since 1932 *Job* has been a regular feature of the programmes presented by the Vic-Wells, later the Sadler's Wells, Ballet, the part of Satan usually being danced by Mr. Robert Helpmann, and the theme of Blake's vision has thus been revealed in material form to many. thousands of his countrymen and even to other peoples.

As this book is going through the press the whole ballet is being drastically revised by the choreographer for its first production at the Royal Opera House, Covent Garden, in June, 1948, with a new *décor* designed by Mr. John Piper.

[A piano version of the music by Vally Lasker was published by the Oxford University Press in 1931. The full score was published by the same Press in 1939. A rendering on gramophone records was issued by "His Master's Voice" in 1946.]

XV

THORNTON'S "VIRGIL"

THE SPLENDOUR of Blake's *Illustrations of the Book of Job* might have set him once and for all upon a pedestal from which he would never again look down to consider a trivial or ill-paid commission; but Blake had by now learnt that humility became him and his art better than pride, so that he was able to turn from the *Book of Job* and loose the full vigour of his mind upon making a series of illustrations for Dr. Robert John Thornton's *Pastorals of Virgil*. Dr. Thornton was family physician to the Linnells. He had studied medicine at Cambridge and Guy's Hospital and began practice in London in 1797. His main interest, however, was botany, and while continuing in practice as a physician, he adventured on a lavish scale in publishing botanical works. He lost heavily in some of these ventures, but he was both industrious and versatile, and published books on several other subjects, including a school *Virgil* in 1812. This was at first unadorned, illustrations being published separately in 1814. A second edition with these woodcut illustrations was published in 1819, and its success was such that a third edition was planned for publication in 1821. Owing to Thornton's association with the Linnells, it came about that in 1820 Blake was introduced to his notice with the suggestion that he should assist in illustrating the new edition of the *Virgil*. Blake was not, however, to be employed only as designer of illustrations. He was to work also, perhaps primarily, as journeyman engraver, and in this capacity he drew and engraved on

copper a set of six plates showing portrait busts of Theocritus,
Virgil, Augustus Caesar, Agrippa, Julius Caesar and Epicurus.
He also made a drawing after Nicolas Poussin's painting of
"The Giant Polypheme", and from this a wood-engraving was
executed by Byfield. These engravings possess no artistic merit
whatever, and Dr. Thornton evidently intended them only as
adjuncts to the main mass of illustration, which consisted of no
less than 117 pages of small woodcuts. Most of these are puerile
in quality and are unsigned, though the artists included Bewick,
Byfield, Hughes, Thompson and Thurston. Some had already
appeared in the earlier editions, others were newly designed or
engraved, and all of them no doubt helped to render the book
more palatable to a juvenile audience than if it had been without
them. The volumes were entitled:

*The Pastorals of Virgil, with a Course of English Reading, Adapted
for Schools: in which all The Proper Facilities are given, enabling youth
to acquire The Latin Language in the Shortest Period of Time. Illustrated
by 230 Engravings.*

They were printed by J. M'Gowan and published by F. C. and
J. Rivingtons in association with a number of other publishers,
and were sold in a pink sheepskin binding at 15s. (with a full
Allowance to the Trade and Schoolmasters). An advertisement
card was circulated with the following announcement by Mr.
Harrison, agent for Dr. Thornton:

Dr. Thornton's Greatly admired and esteemed *Virgil* illustrated by
two hundred and thirty cuts! Engraved by the first Artists of this
Country is now on Sale & may be purchased of W. Harrison, Wine
Merchant Nº. 13 Little Tower Street, London. This work is patronized by the Master of St. Paul's.

The book has a faint attraction at the present time for connoisseurs of "period" pieces, though this would not entitle it to any

more attention than many similar productions. Its only source of value and importance is, in fact, to be found in Blake's contribution to the 230 illustrations. To him was assigned the task of illustrating an "Imitation" of Virgil's first Eclogue by the early eighteenth-century poet, Ambrose Phillips, in which two shepherds, Colinet and Thenot, engage in a mild "pastoral" dialogue. Blake had never before executed any wood-engravings, and his preliminary designs gave no hint of what the final result would be. He filled a small oblong sketch-book with faint pencil drawings touched with sepia which have a delicate beauty of their own, and the contrast between these and their counterparts on wood is startling (Plate 38). Blake always contrived to let his originality play upon any medium in which he chose to work, whether water-colour, tempera, or metal plate, so that the result was distinct from the work of any other artist.

He had not actually engraved on wood before, and the ruggedness of his designs has often been attributed to his ignorance of the technique. He was, however, quite accustomed to working in somewhat similar media. He had himself described the method of how to "woodcut on pewter", and examples of this process may be seen in his designs for Hayley's ballad of *Little Tom, the Sailor*, published in 1800. Many of his relief-etchings on copper also produce very much the same effect as woodcuts, so that his lack of familiarity with the wood-block as a medium has been given an exaggerated importance. This is only saying, however, that Blake probably had a very clear idea of the effect that he wished to produce with his wood-engravings, and does not in any way detract from the grandeur of his achievement. Though superlatives are dangerous, it is impossible to avoid them in writing of Blake's woodcuts. The pages of Thornton's *Virgil* are filled with everything that is trite and trivial. Suddenly, as a leaf is turned, a page of Blake's woodcuts leaps into the consciousness and for a moment the world is transformed by the breath of genius. As the first shock of astonishment passes, the wonder grows at how Blake has conveyed so much in such small compass. Each block as first engraved measured only 35 to 40 × 84 mm., or about $1\frac{1}{2} \times 3\frac{1}{2}$ inches, yet in that tiny space, using the greatest economy of line, Blake has depicted with complete mastery a spacious landscape, a cataclysm of nature, or a tender pastoral scene. The wood-blocks are arranged for the most part close together, four on a page, and each one gains, if possible, by the proximity of the others. The designs do not all reach the same high level, though the least successful is a masterpiece if put beside the work of any other wood-engraver of the period. They are indeed, in nearly all respects, the most completely satisfying woodcuts ever executed, and yet Blake did not ever again choose to make any engravings in the same medium. Linnell's descendants possessed a wood-block[1] on which Blake made a careful pencil and Indian ink drawing of great beauty (Plate 37), representing "The Prophet of Isaiah foretelling the Destruction of Jerusalem", but this was never actually cut. No record exists of his own feelings on the woodcuts. Did he not regard them seriously as works of art, or did he feel that he could never again attain the same level of artistic creation in that particular vein? Probably neither view is true. He was busied in the succeeding years with his engravings of the *Illustrations of the Book of Job*, and had no occasion to turn his attention again to wood-engraving.

Whatever Blake's thoughts about the woodcuts may have been, there can be no doubt of the effect of their impact on the consciousness of his contemporaries. Dr. Thornton was not an imaginative man. He was enterprising and prolific where botany

[1] Now in the Print Room of the British Museum.

and medicine were concerned, and employed recognized artists to illustrate his works, sometimes on a lavish scale. Unrecognized genius, however, left him unimpressed, and Blake's woodcuts only prompted him to jeer. When they were laid before him he was horrified by such rough and amateurish work, and immediately gave directions that the designs should be recut by a professional wood-engraver. This would have been done but for the intercession of Linnell, and, it is said, of Sir Thomas Lawrence and James Ward, whom Thornton happened to meet at the house of a common friend. Though these artists warmly praised the woodcuts, Thornton remained uneasy, and felt that he had to apologize for the inclusion of such work in his book. Accordingly he caused the following note to be printed below the first woodcut:

The Illustrations of this English Pastoral are by the famous BLAKE, the illustrator of *Young's* Night Thoughts, and *Blair's* Grave; who designed and engraved them himself. This is mentioned, as they display less of art than genius, and are much admired by some eminent painters.

Three of the designs, Nos. 14-16, were actually re-engraved for the book by a professional hand, and lost all character and merit in the process. Fortunately they are the least important of the series. A fourth was also recut, presumably by the same hand, and the result is an interesting example of how the originality of genius may be reduced to the conventional formula of the moment. It was not used in the book but was printed side by side with an impression from Blake's corresponding wood-block in *The Athenaeum* for January 21, 1843, and this print is reproduced here (Plate 39). The writer of this article was reviewing an edition of *The Vicar of Wakefield*, illustrated by William Mulready, who had, however, not executed the wood-engravings himself, and took the opportunity to protest vigorously against the almost universal practice of having an artist's drawings engraved by a journeyman engraver. Blake's woodcuts were the most convincing argument that he could find against the prevalent mechanization of the art—worse, indeed, in its results than the photographic process reproductions of succeeding years. Dr. Thornton, a cheerful and industrious materialist, could hardly be expected to sympathize with the "artistic" view of his friends, and so tried to cover himself with the statement quoted above. Blake's feelings on reading Thornton's note may be imagined. He had suffered from similar patronage at the outset of his creative career, when the kind friends who helped him to print his early poems in the volume of *Poetical Sketches* in 1783 apologized in a Preface for "the irregularities and defects to be found in almost every page". This situation was now repeated in his old age, and again Blake, still unrepentant, knew that his "irregularities and defects" were the product of the divine imagination that was in him, and must not be altered or revised. He so far forgave Thornton as to execute another small copperplate engraving in 1825 for an unsuccessful "annual" called *Remember Me!* It clearly, however, gave him much satisfaction when he penned in 1827 his pungent marginalia in a copy of Thornton's pamphlet on The Lord's Prayer. "I look upon this", he wrote, "as a Most Malignant & Artful attack upon the Kingdom of Jesus By the Classical Learned, thro' the Instrumentality of Dr. Thornton. The Greek & Roman Classics is the Antichrist. I say Is & not Are as most expressive & correct too." He further developed his attack on Thornton as the arch-materialist, and gives near the end his own parody of Thornton's new translation of The Lord's Prayer, heading it: "Doctor Thornton's Tory Translation, Translated out of its disguise in the Classical & School languages into the vulgar English". He concludes: "Thus we see that the Real God is the Goddess Nature, & that God Creates nothing but what can be Touch'd & Weighed & Taxed & Measured; all else is Heresy & Rebellion against Ceasar, Virgil's Only God—see Eclogue i; for all this we thank Dr. Thornton". Blake was very ill and nearing his life's end, but he had not forgotten his woodcuts for the Imitation of Virgil's First Eclogue and how the breath of imagination had ruffled Dr. Thornton's Tory mind.

In 1820 Blake's defenders had been a few eminent and sophisticated persons. Four years later he was to know the greater satisfaction of being almost worshipped by less sophisticated intelligences, when he became the centre of a group of young artists, the chief of whom were Samuel Palmer, Edward Calvert and George Richmond. It was the Virgil woodcuts that affected them beyond everything else, so that Palmer and Calvert themselves made lovely engravings and woodcuts of pastoral subjects bearing the clear inspiration of Blake in every line, and Palmer even made sepia drawings and brilliantly coloured paintings having much of the strength and ruggedness of Blake's woodcuts. In 1824 Palmer wrote in his notebook: "I sat down with Mr. Blake's Thornton's *Virgil* woodcuts before me, thinking to give to their merits my feeble testimony. I happened first to think of their sentiment. They are visions of little dells and nooks and corners of Paradise: models of the exquisitest pitch of intense poetry. I thought of their light and shade, and looking upon them I found no word to describe it. Intense depth, solemnity, and vivid brilliancy only coldly and partially describe them. There is in all such a mystic and dreamy glimmer as penetrates and kindles the inmost soul, and gives complete and unreserved delight, unlike the gaudy daylight of this world. They are like all that wonderful artist's works, the drawing aside

M

of the fleshly curtain, and the glimpse which all the most holy, studious saints and sages have enjoyed, of that rest which remaineth to the people of God." [1]

    .   .   .   .

Blake's woodcuts number seventeen in all, together with three blocks engraved from his designs by another hand. The first woodcut is larger than the others, and was printed by itself as a frontispiece to Philips's Eclogue. Below it is the note by Dr. Thornton already quoted. No preliminary design for this block is extant, but the sketch-book formerly in the Linnell collection contained drawings for the other nineteen designs with one extra drawing (No. 4) which was not used. The sketch-book was sold with the Linnell collection at Christie's on March 15, 1918 (lot 205, Parsons, £113), and was afterwards traded to America. It was sold again by the American Art Association, New York, on April 22, 1924 (lot 60, $1,625), being bought by the Brick Row Bookshop Inc. The drawings were then sold separately, and are now in the possession of several collectors. Sixteen of them, by the courtesy of their owners, were photographed for reproduction by the Nonesuch Press, which first used them in *The Pencil Drawings of William Blake*, 1927, and again in *Blake's Illustrations for Thornton's Virgil*, 1937. The reproductions, which are the size of the originals, included the unused drawing, but did not include the drawings for four of the woodcuts (Nos. 5, 7, 12, 18), as photographs of these could not be obtained.

The wood-blocks for all except the first as made by Blake measured 35 to 40 × 84 mm., but they were found to be somewhat too large for the pages of the *Virgil* and were ruthlessly cut down before they were printed, losing about 5 × 10 mm. Proofs

---

[1] *Life and Letters of Samuel Palmer*, by A. H. Palmer (London, 1892), p. 15.

taken by Blake before the blocks were mutilated shew that he intended them to be printed four together just as they appear in the book. Very few examples of these proofs are in existence. Two sheets with Nos. 2-5 and 6-9 are in the British Museum Print Room, and one of these is reproduced here (Plate 40). A sheet with the first set is in the collection of the late Frank Rinder, and comparison of this with the sheet in the British Museum shews that further work was done on the blocks after this proof was taken. A sheet with the second set is inserted in the MS. in the Fitzwilliam Museum, Cambridge, known as *An Island in the Moon*. Another sheet of the first set, signed *W. Blake fecit*, was formerly in the possession of Samuel Palmer, and of this he wrote in 1864: "Mr. Blake gave this page to me in Fountain Court: impressions taken there, at his own press, by his own hands, and signed by him under my eyes".[1] It was afterwards in the possession of his son, A. H. Palmer, and was exhibited at the Victoria and Albert Museum in 1926. It is now in the collection of Mr. Philip Hofer. These are the only true proofs that are known at the present time, all having been made, probably by Blake himself, before the blocks were cut down. Other sets of so-called proofs were taken from the blocks after they had been used in the book, and were no doubt distributed to his friends by John Linnell. There exists a receipt written on the back of one of Harrison's advertisement cards showing that the blocks were bought by Linnell in 1825. It runs as follows:

September 16, 1825. Received of Mr. Linnell for the Wood-Blocks executed by Mr. Blake two guineas for Mr. Harrison.

R. I. Thornton, M.D.[2]

[1] Catalogue of an Exhibition of Drawings, Etchings and Woodcuts by Samuel Palmer, etc. Victoria and Albert Museum (1926), p. 28.
[2] *Loc. cit.*

Linnell therefore obtained the blocks for about 2s. 6d. each and may have been making sets of prints for many years after Blake's death. These prints are sometimes on thin paper which gives much better impressions than the rough paper of the *Virgil*, and they are therefore sometimes erroneously described as "early proofs". The blocks remained in the possession of Linnell's descendants, and are in perfect condition. They were lost to sight for many years, but were eventually found among the effects of the late Herbert Linnell, one of the trustees of the Blake-Linnell collections, and were seen by the writer in October 1937 (Plate 36). Permission was obtained from the trustees for electrotypes to be made from the blocks for use in the Nonesuch volume of 1937, and as the quality of the prints thus obtained was the same as if the wood-blocks themselves were to be used, the designs can there again be seen as Blake saw them in 1821. The wood-blocks were sold at Christie's on December 2, 1938, and were bought for the National Art Collections Fund. They are now safely housed in the Print Room of the British Museum.

The woodcuts were first reproduced and published by Thomas B. Mosher, Portland, Maine, in 1899. They were reproduced again with an introduction by Laurence Binyon for the Unicorn Press, London, in 1902. Enlarged facsimiles in platinotype were made by Frederic H. Evans and issued privately in 1912. The two sheets of proofs were reproduced side by side with the prints as they appeared in the book in the *Burlington Magazine*, December 1920.

XVI

"THE PILGRIM'S PROGRESS"

THE PLAIN ENGLISH NAMES of John Bunyan and William Blake had not occurred in any sort of conjunction in a book before the year 1941. The name of one does not inevitably recall that of the other, in the way that those of Milton and Blake have come to be associated. Yet Bunyan and Blake, separated in time by almost the same interval that lies between Milton and Blake, have much in common. Both were artists in their different ways, both were poets singing at first in spontaneous, rude strains, with an apparent simplicity of purpose. Both arose from obscure origins by the strength of their personalities and intellects. Both became religious visionaries, who dreamed dreams and worked for the Redemption of Man by means of their writings. A striking difference lies in their methods of working. Bunyan spoke in a language that could be readily understood by his fellow men, and rose to a contemporary pre-eminence through the immediate popularity of his writing and preaching. Blake, on the other hand, chose to deliver most of his message in a deliberately cryptic language, filled with mannerisms, which baffled his contemporaries and is only now, more than a hundred years after his death, coming to be more fully understood. Bunyan again needed a "conversion" to bring his artistry to fruition. Blake pursued the course of artistic creation coupled with religious fervour throughout his long life, and needed no conversion to open the gates of his mind to inspiration from the spiritual world. Perhaps the greatest quality possessed by Bunyan and Blake in common was the complete integrity of their minds, maintained by both in the face of material hardships and lack of worldly possessions.

The first edition of Bunyan's *Pilgrim's Progress* was printed in London, and was entered at Stationer's Hall on December 22, 1677. It was licensed on February 18, 1678. A second edition was published in the same year, and a third in 1679. The first two editions were not illustrated. The third was provided with a frontispiece representing the author lying asleep above the "Denn" where he dreamed his dream. There can be no doubt that he meant thereby to indicate the confined space of the Bedford gaol where his allegory first came to his mind. The illustrator, however, interpreted the "Denn" more literally and provided it with a lion, which has otherwise no particular significance. This was afterwards adopted as the traditional form of the frontispiece, and for more than 250 years *The Pilgrim's Progress* has seldom appeared without the embellishment of the Dreamer with his apparently tame lion lying in a cave below him. It was to the fifth edition, published in 1680, that illustrations in the ordinary sense were added. This edition was given a portrait of Bunyan, a representation of the burning of the Faithful, and "Thirteen Copper Cuts curiously Engraven for such as desire them", these being charged 1s. extra. Innumerable later editions had illustrations of one kind or another. The subject lent itself to the "chap-book" style of illustration with many small and rough woodcuts or copper plates. No artist of great distinction attempted the task of illustrating Bunyan in the eighteenth century until it was undertaken by Thomas Stothard in 1788. In the nineteenth century numerous book-illustrators tried their hands, among others Turner, Cruikshank, David Scott, Holman Hunt,

Gordon Browne and Strang. Some of their designs were engraved on wood by the most celebrated craftsmen of the period,
often with charming effect. In no instance, however, were the
refined productions of a Stothard or a pre-Raphaelite artist
suited to the plain style of Bunyan's writing. The rough and
homely woodcuts of a chap-book are more in tune with the
tinker-preacher's spontaneous art than the polished products of
the sophisticated book-illustrator.

When my grandfather, Dr. John Brown, then Minister of
the Church at Bunyan Meeting in Bedford, was writing his
standard *Life of Bunyan* (first published in 1885), he was un-
easily aware of this deficiency in the pictorial representation of
Bunyan's allegory. He was moved to suggest that "an ideally
perfect *Pilgrim's Progress* would have been the Pilgrim story
by Bunyan with illustrations by Albrecht Dürer or Hans
Holbein". Dr. Brown was naturally bringing to his mind the
greatest artists of the past who had a creative faculty comparable
with Bunyan's, and a capacity for simple representation of allegory such as is found in Holbein's Dance of Death. There was
no name of Bunyan's time or later which suggested itself to him,
and this is not surprising because in 1885 the one artist since
Bunyan's day who had possessed all the necessary qualities was
known only to a few, and even to them connoted eccentricity,
or even madness, rather than a transcendent genius fit to be
placed beside that of the author of *The Pilgrim's Progress*.

William Blake, born nearly seventy years after Bunyan's
death, can now be seen in his true proportions, and it is evident
that he can stand beside Bunyan with undiminished stature, and
that many parallels can be found between their minds and art.
Blake's art became much more highly intellectualized than
Bunyan's, but he never became sophisticated, and although he

was a painter of the highest originality he could also, when he chose, bend his mind to illustrate the work of another with almost literal attention to detail. During his earlier years Blake worked chiefly as the engraver of designs by others, among these being many by Thomas Stothard and John Flaxman. He also illustrated a few small books with his own designs, such as Mary Wollstonecraft's *Original Stories from Real Life*, 1791. His first big venture as an illustrator was the series of 537 large water-colour designs for Young's *Night Thoughts*, begun about 1795, and partly engraved in 1797. This was followed about 1801 by 114 water-colour drawings for the *Poems* of Thomas Gray, none of which were engraved. For many years after this Blake's main output as an illustrator was concerned with the works of Milton. Nearly every one of Milton's major poems, except *Samson Agonistes*, was furnished with a set of elaborate water-colour drawings, and several of these were done more than once. Particularly notable are the magnificent sets of designs illustrating *Paradise Lost* and *Paradise Regained*, which by themselves prove Blake to have supreme qualities as the translator of poetical conceptions into the realm of vision. Finally, during the last years of his life, Blake was engaged on his most celebrated works, the *Illustrations of the Book of Job* and the unfinished series of over 100 large designs for Dante's *Inferno*, upon which he was working at the time of death in 1827.

Knowledge of Blake's tastes and interests would at once suggest that he must have been familiar for most of his life with Bunyan's *Pilgrim's Progress*. Its allegorical and visionary qualities would have attracted him from an early age; he was a precocious reader, and, once he had given his attention to a work of outstanding merit, he did not forget it. Yet there is no reference to Bunyan anywhere in Blake's extant writings. The

earliest evidence of any awareness of *The Pilgrim's Progress* is to
be found in a very beautiful design, a "woodcut on pewter",
known as "Sweeping the Interpreter's House". This has usually
been assigned to about the year 1817, but my recent investigations of all Blake's separate plates have established the fact that
this design was first cut on metal about the year 1794, when
Blake was thirty-seven years old.

It has long been known that, in addition to this single print,
Blake made a series of water-colour drawings illustrating *The
Pilgrim's Progress*. It was recorded by W. M. Rossetti in his list
of Blake's works at the end of the second volume of Gilchrist's
Life of Blake, 1863. Rossetti's entry is as follows:

211 Twenty-eight Designs from the "Pilgrim's Progress." (Mr.
Milnes.) Water-colours often unfinished; one or two little beyond
pencil-sketches.

These are rather small designs, having quite a sufficient measure of
Blake's spirit in them, but much injured by the handiwork of Mrs.
Blake, the colour being untidy-looking and heavy for the most part,
and crude where strength is intended. Two of the designs, at any rate,
may be considered untouched by Mrs. Blake.

(Brief descriptions of the separate designs then follow.)

The entry appears unchanged in the second edition of Gilchrist's
Life, published in 1880.

It is clear, therefore, that Rossetti saw these designs which
were in 1863 in the possession of Richard Monkton Milnes,
afterwards the first Lord Houghton, and father of the late
Marquess of Crewe. Rossetti seems, however, to have considered
that they were of small account as works of art, and is particularly damping in his remarks as to their having been "much
injured by the handiwork of Mrs. Blake". The previous history
of the paintings is unknown, though it is very probable that they

came from the collection of Thomas Butts, much of which was bought by Monkton Milnes.

After his father's death Lord Crewe sold almost the whole of the Blake collection in 1903, and he was uncertain how it came about that the designs for *The Pilgrim's Progress* were not included in the sale. He thought it probable that they were overlooked, as they came to light again some years later on somewhat ragged mounts, in a forgotten drawer; it was then that they were provided with neat mounts and a protective slip-in case. Lord Crewe appreciated the great beauty of the drawings, but he did not draw much attention to them. Few visitors ever asked to see them, so that their existence was largely forgotten. When Lord Crewe first told me of them, about the year 1928, and offered to shew them to me, I was naturally eager to see them, though Rossetti's remarks warned me not to entertain too great expectations as to their merit. Perhaps for this reason, my first impression of them was not very favourable, and I formed the opinion that they did not represent Blake's best work. Ten years later I asked permission from Lord Crewe to renew my acquaintance with the drawings, and on this occasion I saw the necessity for a complete revision of my former views. I began to doubt the justice of Rossetti's strictures on the conjectural spoiling by Mrs. Blake, and I saw instead a magnificent series of designs, of uneven quality as is inevitable among so many, but including some of the loveliest water-colours that Blake had ever made. The colouring in a few was heavy where that particular effect was suited to the subject, but Rossetti's charge that it was "untidy-looking and heavy for the most part" was, I thought, entirely untrue. I soon decided that the designs should be made known, if possible, to a greater number of Blake's admirers, and with Lord Crewe's help the arrangements were concluded by which the Limited

Editions Club of New York was enabled to produce in 1941 an edition of *The Pilgrim's Progress*, illustrated with reproductions of Blake's designs in colour. It had been intended in 1939 to make these reproductions in London and to issue them both in this country and in America. The project was abandoned owing to the second World War, and in 1940 Blake's drawings were sent to New York. They were not brought back after the reproductions had been made, but were exhibited in New York for the benefit of a refugee organization. They are now permanently housed in the Frick Collection in New York.

An examination of the drawings made it possible to determine the approximate date of their execution. The watermark in the paper, wherever it appeared, was that of J. Whatman, associated with various parts of the date 1824. The water-colours cannot, therefore, have been made before that year, and, since Blake was not in the habit of carrying large stocks of drawing paper, but tended rather to buy it as he needed it, it is probable that 1824 was the actual year of their composition. He was at this time still engaged on the engravings for the *Illustrations of the Book of Job*, and he was soon afterwards to embark on his vast series of designs for Dante's *Inferno*. It seems likely that these preoccupations may account for the fact that the *Pilgrim's Progress* series was never finished, and it may be that Thomas Butts, if he possessed it, did not acquire it until after Blake's death, as he would have been unlikely to buy works which Blake had no doubt intended to improve and finish when the opportunity offered itself. This conjecture is made the more probable by another confusion that has arisen concerning the subject of one of the designs, as will presently be described.

The number of water-colour drawings in Lord Crewe's possession was twenty-nine. The number was given by Rossetti as twenty-eight, the difference being accounted for by the fact that he has omitted to mention No. XVII, "Christian in the Arbour". He has applied this title instead to the frontispiece design of the Dreamer asleep in "a certain place where there was a Denn". It may be assumed, therefore, that there were really twenty-nine designs in 1863, when we have the first mention of their existence. A few of the drawings have a word or two scribbled in the margin by Blake. None has any full inscription in his hand, nor is there any signature. All have been numbered and inscribed with a title by a later unknown hand, but these inscriptions carry no authority and I have ignored them in making my own descriptions and arrangements.

The subjects of twenty-eight of the designs and their order is as follows:

I. John Bunyan dreams a Dream. In his first illustration Blake follows the traditional frontispiece which embellished the earlier and many later editions of the book as an engraving or a woodcut. The design is arranged in three horizontal layers. In the centre is the figure of the author in a long blue garment lying asleep beneath a row of massive trees. Below him is the "denn", containing a mildly sleeping lion. The upper layer among the branches of the trees is sketched in with the brush, and indicates some of the incidents of the dream. It is possible to discern Christian setting out on his journey, the combat with Apollyon, and the Gate of Heaven.

The design appears to be finished, the cloudiness of the upper layer being intended to give the effect of dream-land in contrast with the more precise outlines of the sleeper and the lion.

II. Christian reading in his Book. Christian, clothed in rags and with his back turned to the City, is walking in the fields.

He is bowed down by a great burden bound onto his back, and he carries an open book in his hands. Dense clouds obscure the sky, and flames arise from the buildings he is quitting. There is a background of trees.

The design is elaborately finished with strong colours (Plate 41).

III. CHRISTIAN MEETS EVANGELIST. Christian, emerging from the door of his house, meets Evangelist, who carries a scroll in his left hand and with his right points towards the Wicket Gate in the distance. The door of Christian's house is in the form of a Gothic arch. The other buildings in the background have the massive form of Druid temples. These Gothic and Druidical details denote, in Blake's symbolism, the opposed forces of Art and Materialism.

The greater part of the drawing is carefully finished, but some of the details in the figure of Evangelist appear to be unfinished, particularly his right hand.

IV. CHRISTIAN PURSUED BY OBSTINATE AND PLIABLE. Christian is running with outstretched arms from the City of Destruction. Two other figures, Obstinate and Pliable, are in pursuit. Heavy clouds swag over the buildings, which consist of a church with a double spire, a castle with turrets at each corner, and rounded structures without definite form.

The drawing is fully finished in strong colour.

V. CHRISTIAN IN THE SLOUGH OF DESPOND. Christian is floundering across the Slough, while Pliable extricates himself on the side towards the City of Destruction. The buildings of the City show numerous spires, and on the right a huge dome surmounted by a cross. The dome is a symbol derived from St. Paul's Cathedral, which, because of its "mathematic form", denotes mental rigidity, that is, lack of the imaginative faculty. Portentous clouds hang over the scene.

The drawing is fully finished in heavy colouring.

VI. CHRISTIAN DRAWN OUT OF THE SLOUGH BY HELP. The powerful figure of Help stoops over Christian in the Slough and grasps him by his upraised arms. From behind Help a road leads up into the hills, above which is the rising sun.

The figures, particularly that of Christian, are naïvely drawn, much violence being done to anatomical accuracy, but the colouring is fully finished with a strong effect.

VII. CHRISTIAN DIRECTED BY MR. WORLDLY-WISEMAN. Christian crouches intent upon the Book in his hand, and above him stands the massive figure of Mr. Worldly-Wiseman, whose bearded face expresses complacency in every line. With his left hand Mr. Worldly-Wiseman points towards the Hill (Mount Sinai), which flashes fire and smoke from its summit.

The drawing is fully finished.

VIII. CHRISTIAN FALLS AT THE FEET OF EVANGELIST. Christian has fallen on his knees at the feet of Evangelist, who stoops to take him by his right hand and raise him up. The fire and smoke of the Mountain rise in the background.

The drawing is finished.

IX. CHRISTIAN FEARS THE FIRE FROM THE MOUNTAIN. Christian stands in an attitude of awe while fire and thunderbolts play around him.

The drawing is fully finished in brilliant colours (Plate 42).

X. CHRISTIAN KNOCKS AT THE WICKET GATE. Christian steps forward to grasp the knocker on the Gate. This is represented as a door shaped like a Gothic arch in a high wall. Around the door is a faintly indicated design of human figures, and this is overpainted with a halo of rainbow colours. Beyond the Gate rise hills, and above them is the orb of the sun. To Christian's left and behind him is a wall on the edge of which is balanced a bow and arrow. This represents the castle of Beelzebub who seeks to shoot at those entering the Gate. The door itself is inscribed, *Knock And It Shall Be Opened.*

The drawing is finished.

XI. THE GATE IS OPENED BY GOODWILL. Christian with his foot upon the lintel is received by Goodwill, a bearded figure with a nimbus round his head. The design of figures around the door is now more clearly drawn and is of great beauty. There are faint indications of rays of light emanating from Goodwill.

The drawing is finished, though the colouring is pale.

XII. THE MAN IN THE IRON CAGE. Christian and the Interpreter stand on the left, the Interpreter having a large key in his hand. The other half of the picture is occupied by a massive iron grill behind which sits a man fettered by his neck, wrists and ankles. This figure symbolizes the fettered mind as much for the author as for the illustrator.

The figures of Christian and the Interpreter are unfinished, though the cage of Despair and its occupant are fully finished in heavy colours.

XIII. THE MAN WHO DREAMED OF THE DAY OF JUDGEMENT. Christian and the Interpreter stand on the right. In this design, which is fully finished, the Interpreter has a short beard which does not appear in the two preceding designs. The Dreamer sits, with a troubled expression on his face, on the edge of his couch, and over him hang huge and heavy curtains, which imply a sense of impending doom. The colour is correspondingly dark.

XIV. CHRISTIAN BEFORE THE CROSS. Christian stands in adoration before the Cross, represented by Blake as a vision of Christ crucified. The figure of Christ appears in a luminous cloud with rays of light shooting downwards. The shaft of the Cross becomes in its lower part the trunk of a tree, whose roots spread in all directions over the roof of a stone vault—the Sepulchre of the text. Vines are growing up the tree and on either side. Christian's burden has fallen off his back, and is poised on the edge of the vault into which it will tumble.

The drawing is fully finished (Plate 43).

In this lovely design Blake has used the form of an earlier engraving contained in his illuminated book, *Jerusalem*, which was finished in 1818. This plate, known as "Christ crucified adored by Albion", represents Christ nailed to the Tree of Good and Evil, while Albion, or Man, worships from below with arms outstretched so that he is himself in a cruciform attitude. In his interpretation of Bunyan's image Blake has modified the figure of Man, but it is clear that the memory of the plate from *Jerusalem* was in his mind.

XV. CHRISTIAN MET BY THE THREE SHINING ONES. Christian, now represented as clothed in a long garment instead of his rags, and carrying a staff, is on the right of the picture. A vine, such as was seen on either side of the Tree in the last design, is beside him. The Three Shining Ones, in the form of female figures, each with wings and a nimbus, stand before him. One lays her right forefinger on his forehead, and carries a roll with dependent seal in her left hand. Christian's discarded rags hang from the hands of the second and the third—Christian's sins, which have now been forgiven him.

The drawing is finished in delicate colours, which contrast with the heavy colouring of the first part of the pilgrimage.

XVI. CHRISTIAN CLIMBS THE HILL DIFFICULTY. Christian is clambering up steep and jagged rocks, his back and limbs being marked with blood-stains, from the scratches made by the thorns which obstruct his path. At the top of the rocks is a pent-house, indicating the "pleasant Arbour" of the text, "made by the Lord of the Hill for the refreshment of weary Travailers". The drawing is fully finished.

XVII. CHRISTIAN IN THE ARBOUR. Christian, still marked with scratches, is seated on a bench in the Arbour, to which he has returned in search of the Roll. In his right hand he holds the Roll, and he raises his left hand above his head in jubilation and thanks for its recovery. The arbour is made of brightly coloured leaves and flowers, and brilliant rainbow colours arch over it. The whole design, which is carefully finished, pulsates with colour of matchless beauty, thus expressing Christian's feelings of joy and gratitude (Plate 44).

XVIII. CHRISTIAN PASSES THE LIONS. Christian is passing between two rocks with his left arm upraised and a sword in his right hand. On either side, chained to the rock by a foreleg, is a beast, representing a lion according to Blake's convention. Standing above, at the door of the Pilgrim's House, is the Porter calling to Christian not to be afraid of the chained lions. The drawing is finished.

XIX. CHRISTIAN GOES FORTH ARMED. On the right of the picture is Christian, with a sword in his left hand, and a shield buckled to his left arm. In his right hand is the Roll. By his side, with an admonishing hand uplifted, is Prudence, a female figure with long hair. Behind them is the doorway of the Armory, indicated by a row of six spears shewing at the top of the doorway. A figure stands beside the door, and two others, one seated, are seen within. These are perhaps Christian's three other friends, Discretion, Pity and Charity.

Parts of this design are roughly sketched, and its interpretation is to some extent conjectural. The earlier numbering of the drawings called this No. 12, and placed the scene in the House of the Interpreter. But the fact that Christian is not clothed in rags and carries a sword shows that this is certainly not Blake's intention.

XX. CHRISTIAN BEATEN DOWN BY APOLLYON. Apollyon, painted in lurid colours, is covered with fishes' scales and has dragon's wings, as described in the text: thunderbolts issue from his mouth. His legs are straddled over his opponent who has been beaten to his knees, and his uplifted arms are holding darts with which he is about to deliver the final blows. Christian defends himself with the shield on his left arm, and his right hand is about to raise his sword from the ground. The drawing is fully finished.

Apollyon in this drawing, which has a distinctly Chinese effect, is more grotesque than terrible, although he conforms in most respects with the conception of Satan which Blake had already used with better effect in many earlier paintings and engravings.

XXI. FAITHFUL'S NARRATIVE. The figures in this drawing are lightly sketched in pencil, only the background being worked with colour. Christian and Faithful walk together in discourse. Two of the incidents of Faithful's narrative are represented by small but vigorous sketches enclosed in circles at the top of the drawing. On the left hand Faithful is twitched back by the Old Adam taking hold of his flesh. On the right hand he is smitten to the ground by Moses.

XXII. Vanity Fair. The greater part of this design is sketched in pencil, only the two central figures being washed with colour. These figures, representing two of the rabble, are dressed as mountebanks and are performing antics before a pedestal on which Christian and Faithful are standing, with indications of chains hanging from their wrists. Behind the pedestal is a large dome surmounted by a ball elevated on a stem. On each side of the accusers are two onlookers. The front figure of each pair is a woman holding a mask near her face. The hinder figures are very roughly sketched, but that on the left hand suggests an ecclesiastic wearing a mitre, that on the right a crowned man, these being Blake's usual symbols of the authority of Church and State (Plate 45).

XXIII. Faithful's Martyrdom. On the left hand the body of Faithful is seen consuming in the fire, while his living form is springing upwards to the right with the celestial horses. The dome and cross of the previous design are seen behind the flames of the martyr's pyre. Several onlookers, who are only sketched in, fall prostrate in terror at the spectacle. Christian stands awestruck in the centre with uplifted hands, and his new companion, Hopeful, kneels at his feet.

XXIV. Christian and Hopeful in Doubting Castle. The two Pilgrims crouch in misery on the dungeon floor at the foot of the huge door. Giant Despair lowers over them, his keys hanging from his right hand.

The drawing is finished.

XXV. Christian and Hopeful escape from Doubting Castle. The iron gate of the castle is open, and the two Pilgrims are running away towards the left. Giant Despair, his limbs failing him, leans against the gate-post. His huge crab-tree cudgel is held nervelessly in his left hand.

The drawing is finished (Plate 46).

XXVI. The Pilgrims meet the Shepherds of the Delectable Mountains. The drawing is very unfinished, and is of the simplest possible design. The two Pilgrims, one with a staff, stand on the right facing a group of four shepherds, each in a long robe and a round hat, with a crook shewing above his head. Sheep crop the grass between their feet.

XXVII. Christian and Hopeful in the River. This drawing is only indicated by pencil sketches and a few light touches of colour. On the right the Pilgrims are immersed in the river. Christian with his head just above the water is supported by Hopeful, who points with his right hand to the opposite bank, where there is a group of Shining Ones waiting to receive them.

XXVIII. Christian and Hopeful at the Gates of Heaven. The two Pilgrims with right hands upraised are stepping forwards, guarded on either side by an angel with wings spread so as to meet in an arch above their heads. In the upper part of the design is seen the heavenly host welcoming them with trumpets. Heaven itself is represented by a row of pointed towers, with a single dome surmounted by a cross on the right, indicating that there is forgiveness in Heaven even for the fettered mind of the materialist.

The lovely colour and movement of this design forms a vision of extraordinary beauty and it is a fitting climax with which to end the Dream. The greater part of the design is not rendered in much detail, and it seems as if someone of inferior skill, wishing for greater precision in the central figures, had filled in their features with ink or dark paint. The faces of these four figures have thus become foolish, and indeed almost puerile, in their drawing, but this painful impression is soon lost in contemplating the general beauty of the drawing.

Six of the designs are reproduced here (Plates 41-46) by courtesy of the Director of the Frick Collection, New York.

It will be noticed that the above description of the designs does not account for one of the original twenty-nine. This one I have omitted because a careful examination of its subject has convinced me that it has been mistakenly included in the series, perhaps, as already suggested, owing to its having been bought by Thomas Butts from Mrs. Blake after her husband's death. The subject of the design which I have set aside is given by the annotator as "Christ delivers Faithful from Moses". Rossetti describes it as "Christian beset by Demons in the Valley of the Shadow of Death". The true description of the subject appears to me to be as follows:

On the left a Christ-like figure in a long robe and with a star-shaped nimbus behind his head turns his back on the naked apparition of an old man, which rushes down in flames from the sky and is about to raise a large stone from the ground in its hands. Several heads are dimly indicated in the smoke and clouds hanging about the feet of the apparition. There are jagged mountains and trees in the background. Faithful is nowhere to be seen, and the supposed figure of Christian exactly resembles Blake's representation of Christ Himself in other designs. The naked apparition raising a stone from the ground is clearly Satan, and the whole scene undoubtedly depicts The First

Temptation, with the Spirits of Hunger crowding about Satan's feet. It is, in fact, a rejected design for *Paradise Regained*—rejected because another quite different version which agreed more closely with the text was eventually included in that series. The drawing also differs from all the others in the *Pilgrim's Progress* series in that the paper has been cut round close to the margin and then mounted on another piece of paper. Furthermore, its careful technique and finish approximate more nearly to those of the *Paradise Regained* series than to *The Pilgrim's Progress*. As in many of the former, the effect of the colour has been heightened with gold, which is nowhere used in *The Pilgrim's Progress*.

I have therefore seen no alternative to removing this very beautiful drawing from the series with which it has been so long associated. It was, however, reproduced in the Limited Editions Club volume so that readers might form their own opinion of the propriety of this decision.

Blake's characteristics as a designer are well seen in these water-colours. His use of symmetry is conspicuous, though nowhere carried to excess. His piling on of heavy colour where the subject is one of terror or gloom is a somewhat obvious trick, but he is here conforming to the idiom of the book itself. Bunyan did not seek to produce his effect by subtle gradations of mood, but tried rather to win his readers' ear by direct and unmistakable assault. Blake's lurid passages provide, too, an admirable foil for his flights of more celestial vision such as "Christian at the Wicket Gate", "Christian and Hopeful at the Gates of Heaven", and, beyond all, "Christian in the Arbour". Colour so lovely as this has seldom been achieved by any artist, even by Blake himself, and in this design Blake has expressed, in his old age, all the joy and exuberance of youth and life and beauty. In the unfinished drawings, such as "Vanity Fair" and "Christian and Hopeful in the River", the bones of the designs are so beautiful that it is difficult to believe that Blake did not intentionally leave them incomplete, having seen that they were good. In many of the individual drawings of this series Blake has indeed worked with his divine inspiration in full flight, even though he may have occasionally in others come rather heavily to earth.

Appraisal of the series of designs as a whole is difficult when the separate constituents are so various. Blake has respected Bunyan in that he has illustrated his allegory with careful attention to the details of the narrative. He has not tried to be "original" in his choice of subjects, but has chosen for the most part the same ones that had struck the fancy of the first illustrator in the seventeenth century, even venturing his own version of the traditional frontispiece. Nevertheless he has placed the stamp of his own mind and individuality on every one of the series. Some may have a little too much of his mannerisms, others have been given a touch of his own peculiar symbolism; yet it can be claimed that Blake has interpreted perfectly the spirit of *The Pilgrim's Progress*, and that he has matched Bunyan's genius with his own.

XVII

"REMEMBER ME!"

IN THE EARLY PART of the nineteenth century the pocket
Annual, published each year towards the Christmas festival,
was a well-established publishers' event. *The Amulet, The Keep-
sake, Friendship's Offering, Forget-me-not* are the names of a
few. *The Bijou* was another published by William Pickering in
the years 1828–30. Some of these maintained their popularity
for many years, though they are not now among the second-
hand booksellers' more saleable goods, unless they happen to
contain, as a few of the volumes do, pieces attributed to names
such as Coleridge or Charles Lamb.

Reference has already been made to the many activities of
Dr. Robert John Thornton in the publishing of books, both
splendid and obscure. One of the least known of these and, it
seems, one of the least successful, was a Christmas Annual entitled *Remember Me! A New Years Gift or Christmas Present*,
which appeared before Christmas 1824, but then incontinently
died and was no more seen. This single volume for 1825 is now
a rarity, and would probably have been forgotten were it not
that among its pages Blake made one of his most incongruous
appearances.

The frontispiece depicts a head of the Princess Charlotte
emerging from clouds below which is the legend: *A TRIBUTE
OF REGARD* | *Presented by* | *Your Affectionate Friend* | . . . .
The book consists of a very large number of miscellaneous items

of prose and verse on 336 pages followed by eight pages of engraved music and a *Kalendar | and | Album | 1825. | Dedicated | to | Friendship | and | Superior Intellect*. The *Album* consists of twelve leaves of Whatman paper left blank for the contributions by the Superior Intellect and her friends. They have usually remained blank. The volume ends with twelve pages of print giving lists of *Bankers in London and Westminster, Terms and Returns in 1825, Bank Holidays and Transfer Days, Sovereign Princes of Europe* and *Courts of Law*.

A few of the pieces are by well-known authors, such as Lord Byron, Sir Walter Scott, Miss Elizabeth Carter and Christopher Smart, but the majority are unsigned. Many are informative, others are grave or gay. Gaiety is typified by the following *Anecdote of a Clergyman*: Dr. Wall, a pious minister, was never known to be out of temper. On Sunday, after praying for rain, his servant at dinner dropped some glasses on the floor, whereupon the doctor observed, "We shall have rain now, for I see the *glass* is *low*".

Interspersed among the gems of literature are three copperplate engravings and eight charming coloured prints of flowers. Four of the coloured plates are apparently from drawings by Miss Thornton. The other four are of some interest, as they are miniature versions of plates from Dr. Thornton's celebrated *Temple of Flora*, 1799, one of the most magnificent botanical works ever published. These plates represent "Snow Drop", "Night Blowing Cereus", "Nodding Renealmia", and "Dragon Arum", all being *Tinted by T. Dales*. These miniatures are necessarily less splendid than the originals which were published in an elephant folio, on plates which were not merely portraits of flowers, some of them being suitably embellished. The "Night Blowing Cereus", for example, has *The Flower by Reinagle* and

"REMEMBER ME!"

Moonlight by Pether; but in *Remember Me!* the moonlight is left to the imagination.

Dr. Thornton spared no expense, and expended much ingenuity, in making his little Annual attractive. It is sometimes difficult to justify the acquisition by one collector of several copies of a rare book. During the last twenty-five years six copies of *Remember Me!* in original condition have come to my notice, and I am not ashamed to confess that five of them are now in my library,[1] for, owing to Dr. Thornton's ingenuity, they are all different. The book was usually bound in boards and enclosed in a slip-case of thin card, on one side of which is a pretty scene, stencilled in colours, of children gleaning. The stencilling, being done by hand, is never quite the same, and pleasing variety is introduced by changes in the colours of the binding, the end-papers, and the slip-case. Thus the six copies are dressed as follows:

1. Cream boards, brown end-papers (no slip-case).
2. Cream boards, pink end-papers, bright green case.
3. Brown paper sides, slate-grey end-papers and case.
4. Pink boards, slate-grey end-papers, pink case, with roan strip and gilt lettering on one "spine".
5. Bright green boards, brown end-papers, red case.
6. Pale green boards, orange end-papers, red case.

It was in these surroundings that Blake made his last appearance as a commercial engraver, no doubt being pressed by John Linnell to oblige his friend Dr. Thornton, who may have been giving his professional services to one of Linnell's numerous family and was thus deserving some recompense. Blake had

---

[1] The sixth copy was recently secured by Mr. Douglas Cleverdon.

made a large water-colour drawing[1] representing the "Hiding of the infant Moses in the bulrushes". The mother, supported by her husband, is swooning with emotion, while her husband's sister keeps a look-out on a stone jetty in the background. The atmosphere of Egypt is sustained by a small sphinx crouching on the jetty and pyramids in the background. A palm tree overshadows the group at the river's brink. The incident is described in four pages of text (pp. 32-35), probably from the pen of Miss Thornton, in the course of which the (possibly reluctant) painter may have been appeased by the passage: "None but an artist possessing the imagination and abilities of Mr. Blake could possibly accomplish a task so replete with difficulty that made a painter, when he was trying to represent a father sacrificing his daughter, cover his head in a mantle, feeling that the subject was beyond his power of depicting it". The writer of the article leaves to the reader the decision as to whether it was the painter that covered his own head or made the father in his picture do so. Blake, at any rate, did neither, but executed a lovely engraving, 7 × 10 cm., from his painting, and signed it *Blake del. et sculpt.* This was inserted in *Remember Me!* facing page 34, and immediately invested the commonplace little book with its only real claim to distinction, and that of a high order. It seems that Blake first made his plate somewhat too large, for an apparently unique impression[2] of it, before it was cut down and the lettering altered from *W. Blake invin. & sculp.*, is now in the Lessing J. Rosenwald collection in the National Gallery of Art at Washington (Plate 47).

It has been mentioned that no more was heard of *Remember*

---

[1] Sold with the Linnell collection at Christie's, March 15, 1918, lot 156 (Robson, £120 : 5s.). Now in the H. E. Huntington Library, California.
[2] Exhibited at the Philadelphia Museum of Art, 1939 (No. 233 in the catalogue).

Me! after the first volume had appeared. In my collection, how-ever, is evidence that a second volume may have been in pre-paration, Blake having again been induced to employ his genius in the service of Dr. Thornton. This evidence is in the shape of a tiny sepia drawing, a miniature version of one of his most dramatic and splendid designs, "The Body of Abel found by Adam and Eve; Cain, who was about to bury it, fleeing from the face of his parents". This water-colour drawing was included in Blake's Exhibition of 1809 (*Descriptive Catalogue*, No. xi) and was afterwards in the Linnell collection.[1] A more elaborate version, painted in tempera on a panel, was in the Butts collection and now belongs to Mr. W. Graham Robertson. The miniature in sepia, with variations in detail, came also from the Linnell collection, but was never seen until after the death of the last trustee, Herbert Linnell, from whose effects it came into the hands of Messrs. Robinson of Pall Mall and so into my collection. It measures only 5.5×6.0 cm., and is squared in pencil for en-graving, though it was not actually executed so far as is known (Plate 48).

It is considerably smaller than the "Hiding of Moses", but for this reason would go upright instead of sideways on the page of *Remember Me!* if, as seems very probable, it was intended for the second volume (for 1826) which would have been issued at the end of 1825. Blake was then completely absorbed, between bouts of illness, in his designs for Dante's *Inferno*, and cannot have regretted being released from further obligations to the egregious Dr. Thornton.

[1] Sold at Christie's, March 15, 1918, lot 157 (Sabin, £105).

BIBLIOGRAPHY

BIBLIOGRAPHY
OF WRITINGS BY GEOFFREY KEYNES ON BLAKE

1910 "WILLIAM BLAKE'S LAUGHING SONG: A NEW
VERSION."
Notes and Queries. New Series II, London, September 24,
pp. 241-42.

1910 REVIEWS OF WICKSTEED'S "BLAKE'S JOB" AND
CHESTERTON'S "WILLIAM BLAKE".
The Cambridge Review, December 1, pp. 169-70.

1919 "A TEXTUAL POINT IN BLAKE."
Letter concerning a reading in the "Mad Song".
The Times Literary Supplement, October 23.

1920 "WILLIAM BLAKE AND THE PORTLAND VASE."
Letter.
The Times Literary Supplement, July 3.

1921 A BIBLIOGRAPHY OF WILLIAM BLAKE.
New York: The Grolier Club. 28 cm., pp. xvi + 516 + [10].
4 reproductions in chromo-lithograph, 40 in collotype and 12
in line in the text. 250 copies printed for the Grolier Club on
Hodgkinson's handmade paper, blue quarter-morocco, cloth
sides. (25 copies were distributed to libraries in Great Britain.)

1923 ON THE MORNING OF CHRIST'S NATIVITY.
Milton's Hymn, with unpublished drawings by William
Blake.
With a note on the illustrations.

BIBLIOGRAPHY

Cambridge University Press. 28 cm., pp. 32. 6 illustrations in collotype. ¼ cloth, with Italian paper sides.
150 copies were printed on handmade paper, in ¼ vellum with cloth sides and Italian end papers.

1923 "BLAKE'S MILTON."
The Times Literary Supplement, December 18.

1924 "THE MACGEORGE BLAKES."
The Times Literary Supplement, June 26.

1925 THE WRITINGS OF WILLIAM BLAKE.
London: The Nonesuch Press.
3 volumes. 27·5 cm., Vol. I, pp. xviii + [ii] + 364 + [4], frontispiece in photogravure and 28 illustrations in collotype. Vol. II, pp. vii + [i] + 397 + [3], 10 illustrations in collotype. Vol. III, pp. vii + [i] + 430 + [2], 20 illustrations in collotype.
1500 copies printed on Vidalon handmade paper, and 75 copies on Oxford India paper.

1925 "BLAKE DRAWINGS."
Letter concerning spurious drawings in Figgis's *Paintings of Wm. Blake.*
The Times Literary Supplement, December 17.

1926 LETTERS FROM WILLIAM BLAKE TO THOMAS BUTTS.
Printed in Facsimile, with an Introductory Note.
26·5 cm. Oxford: At the Clarendon Press. 350 copies printed.

1926 MILTON'S POEMS IN ENGLISH. With Illustrations by William Blake.
2 volumes. 25 cm. London: The Nonesuch Press. Vol. I, pp. [viii] + 359. Vol. II, pp. [vi] + 283.

53 illustrations in collotype chosen, edited and annotated. 1450 copies printed on Van Gelder rag paper, bound in quarter parchment, and 90 copies in one volume on Oxford India paper, bound in whole limp vellum or niger morocco.

1926 "WILLIAM BLAKE" with a selection from his poems.
In *Great Names*, an Anthology of English and American Literature. Ed. W. J. Turner.
25·5 cm. New York: The Dial Press, pp. 114-20.

1926 "THE NONESUCH MILTON."
Letter. *The Nation*, September 18.

1926 "WILLIAM BLAKE AND JOSIAH WEDGWOOD."
With unpublished correspondence between Blake and Wedgwood.
The Times Literary Supplement, December 9.

1927 CENTENARY EXHIBITION.
"Books and Prints." Introduction and catalogue.
Burlington Fine Arts Club. *Catalogue of the Blake Centenary Exhibition*, pp. 50-59.
29 cm. London: Privately printed.

1927 POETRY AND PROSE OF WILLIAM BLAKE. Complete in 1 volume.
19·5 cm., London: The Nonesuch Press.
Centenary edition. pp. xii + 1152.
First impression (6500 copies) August 1927.
Second edition, corrected, November 1927.
Third edition, corrections and additions, January 1932.
Fourth edition, reset, April 1939 (reprinted several times).

1927 PENCIL DRAWINGS BY WILLIAM BLAKE.
25 cm. Edited for the Nonesuch Press [London] pp. [ii] +

xvi + 168, with 82 reproductions in collotype. Introduction, and annotation to each drawing. 1550 copies printed.

1927 BLAKE'S ILLUSTRATIONS TO YOUNG'S *NIGHT THOUGHTS*.
Thirty reproductions with Introductory Essay.
41 cm. Harvard University Press. Sold by Oxford University Press.
Pp. [20] + 30 loose leaves. In portfolio. 500 copies printed.

1928 "A GIFT TO THE NATION. BLAKE DRAWINGS FROM THE U.S.A."
The Times, July 28.
Article on the illustrations to Young's *Night Thoughts*, with leading article and reproductions.

1929 "WILLIAM BLAKE."
Article in the *Encyclopaedia Britannica*, 13th edition.

1930 " BLAKE AND HAYLEY. A NEW LETTER."
The Times Literary Supplement, July 31.

1933 "THE TEXT OF BLAKE'S 'A FAIRY SAT UPON MY KNEE'."
Letter.
Notes and Queries. Vol. 165, No. 17, October 28, p. 302.

1933 "DESCRIPTION OF BLAKE'S 'ENTOMBMENT'."
The Vasari Society for the Reproduction of Drawings by Old and Modern Masters. Second Series, part xiv. Oxford University Press.

1935 BLAKE'S ILLUSTRATIONS OF THE BOOK OF JOB.
39 cm. New York: The Pierpont Morgan Library. Introduction, with Laurence Binyon.

112 plates. 500 copies printed (200 for England). In six
fascicles enclosed in a cloth box.

1935 THE NOTEBOOK OF WILLIAM BLAKE called the
Rossetti Manuscript.
Introduction, with reprint of the text from the Nonesuch
edition of the *Writings*.
22·5 cm. London: The Nonesuch Press.
Pp. xii + 163 + 120 collotype plates. 650 copies printed, bound
in blue buckram.

1937 THE ILLUSTRATIONS OF WILLIAM BLAKE FOR
THORNTON'S *VIRGIL*.
Introduction.
23·5 cm. London: The Nonesuch Press.
Pp. 54: with second set of prints in pocket: 1000 copies
printed, bound in linen.
The illustrations printed from electrotypes of the original
wood-blocks.

1939 "BIBLIOGRAPHIE GÉNÉRALE."
Messages, Paris. Volume I, No. 1. pp. 64-68.

1940 "WILLIAM BLAKE."
Cambridge Bibliography of English Literature.
Volume II, pp. 347-350.

1941 THE PILGRIM'S PROGRESS ILLUSTRATED.
With 29 water-color paintings by Wm. Blake . . . with a
new introduction.
Printed at the Spiral Press, New York, for the members of
The Limited Editions Club.
27 cm., pp. [vi] + xxxii + 213 + [7].
29 plates in colour collotype by Jaffe.
Green buckram, label on spine, slip-case.
1500 copies printed.

BIBLIOGRAPHY

1942 "ENGRAVERS CALLED BLAKE."
The Times Literary Supplement, January 17.

1942 "BLAKE'S COPPER-PLATES."
The Times Literary Supplement, January 24.

1942 "WILLIAM BLAKE'S CATALOGUE. A NEW DIS-
COVERY."
The Times Literary Supplement, September 12. With Ruthven
Todd.

1943 "NEW BLAKE DOCUMENTS. HISTORY OF THE
JOB ENGRAVINGS."
The Times Literary Supplement, January 9.

1943 "WILLIAM BLAKE'S BROTHER."
The Times Literary Supplement, February 6, 13.

1943 "NEW LINES FROM BLAKE'S *JERUSALEM*."
The Times Literary Supplement, July 10.

1944 "WILLIAM BLAKE. A MAN WITHOUT A MASK.
BY J. BRONOWSKI."
Time and Tide, June 3. Review.

1945 "BLAKE'S POETICAL SKETCHES."
The Times Literary Supplement, March 10, 17.

1945 "BLAKE." With an Introduction and Notes.
The Faber Gallery. 31 cm., pp. 24, with reproductions of ten
designs in colour.

1945 "BLAKE, TULK, AND GARTH WILKINSON."
The Library, Vol. XXVI, December.

BIBLIOGRAPHY

A note on a private printing of the *Songs of Innocence & of Experience*, 1843.

1947 "THE POETIC VISION."
Review of Northrop Frye's *Fearful Symmetry*.
Time and Tide, December 27, 1947, p. 1394.

IN PREPARATION

THE ENGRAVINGS OF WILLIAM BLAKE.
(Faber and Faber, Ltd.)

THE SEPARATE PLATES OF WILLIAM BLAKE.
(Emery Walker, Ltd.)

THE LETTERS OF WILLIAM BLAKE.
(Rupert Hart-Davis, Ltd.)

A CENSUS OF THE ILLUMINATED BOOKS, REVISED, with Edwin Wolf, 2nd.

THE PAINTINGS AND DRAWINGS OF WILLIAM BLAKE, with Ruthven Todd.
A Catalogue Raisonnée of the whole output.

AN ICONOGRAPHY OF WILLIAM BLAKE.

THE WRITINGS OF WILLIAM BLAKE.
New edition.

INDEX

INDEX

Britannia Triumphant, engraving of, 51
British Museum, Print Room—
  Blake's wood-blocks in, 160, 166
  Descriptive Catalogue in, 80
  Jerusalem in, 161
  Job copper-plates, 134, 143
Broad Street, Golden Square, 4, 41
  Exhibition at, 76, 86
Bronowski, J., 198
Brown, Dr. John, ed. Bunyan, 169
Browne, Gordon, illustrations by, 169
Bryant, Jacob, *New System*, 42, 44, 46, 49
Buckland, J., publisher, 26
Budd & Calkin, Messrs., 143
Bulls of Nineveh, 43
Bunhill Fields, 5
Bunyan, John, 167 ff.
Bunyan, Life of, Brown's, 169
Burlington Fine Arts Club, Centenary Exhibition, 195
  1876 Exhibition, 77
Burlington Magazine, woodcut in, 166
Butcher Hall Lane, 53
Butler, H. T., collection, 36
Butts, Thomas, 29, 31, 34, 79, 118, 119, 124, 141, 190
  Letters to, 194
Butts, Tommy, as engraver, 107
Byfield, Mary, wood-engraving by, 158
Byron, Lord, Blake compared with, 103
  contribution by, 189
Bysshe, Edward, *Art of Poetry*, 15

Cage of Despair, the, 177
"Cain and Abel", Blake's drawing of, 190
Calvert, Edward, 139, 143, 163
Camargo Society, ballet done by, 154, 155
Canterbury Pilgrims, The, 9, 15, 16
  copper-plate of, 106
Carlyle, Alexander, 17
Carnaby Market, 41, 86
Carr, J. Comyns, critic, 65, 66
Carter, Mrs. Elizabeth, 187

Carthew, Miss Alice, collection, 119 n.
Cary, H. F., letter from Coleridge, 95
  and Wainewright, 101
  and Blake, 102
  translation of Dante, 102
Chance, Edward John, print dealer, 141
Chantrey, Francis, 130, 133
Chapman, George, *Homer*, 144
Charles Lamb Society, xii, 84
Chesterton, G. K., on Blake, 193
Chew, Beverly, collection, 35
"Chimney Sweeper", Blake's, 88
Chimney Sweeper's Friend, Montgomery's, 88
Christ crucified, symbolism of, 178
City of Destruction, the, 175
Classical foot, the, 46
Clay and Son, printers, 108
Clements, Dr. James B., 38
Cleverdon, Douglas, 188 n.
Coleridge, S. T., and Blake's *Songs*, 48 n., 95
  his conversation, 99
Colnaghi, print-seller, 119
Colouring, Blake's, 184
Comforters, Job's, 148
Commins's *Elegy*, 45, 57
Cook, John, Wedgwood Museum, 71
Copenhagen, *Job* ballet at, 155
Cortlandt Bishop library, 118
Cosway, Richard, 60
Covent Garden, *Job* ballet at, 156
Cowan, William, collection, 81
Crewe, Marquess of, collection, 118, 124, 141, 171
Croft Murray, Edward, 24
Cruikshank, George, illustrations by, 168
Cumberland, George, 6, 29, 34, 53, 125
  and *Job* engravings, 130
  letter to, 114, 131
Cunliffe, Henry, collection, 116
Cunliffe, Lord, collection, 116
Curtis, Mrs. Greely S., collection, 81

Dales, T., colouring by, 187

202

INDEX

Dante, illustrations to, 102, 106
    copper-plates, 107
    Cary's translation of, 102
    illustrations for, 170, 173
Darwin, Dr. Erasmus, 67
"David delivered out of Many
    Waters", 44
Delectable Mountains, The, 182
Descriptive Catalogue, Blake's, 47,
    76 ff.
    prospectus of, 78
de Valois, Ninette, choreographer, 154
Diaghileff, Serge, 153
Dickinson, John, and Co., paper-
    makers, 24
Dilke, Sir Charles, letter from Linnell
    to, 129
Dobell, P. J., 61 n.
Doctor, The, Southey's, 31, 92
Dodd, Mead and Co., 18
"Dog, The", Blake's engraving of, 89
Dolin, Anton, as "Satan", 155
Doubting Castle, 181
Douce, Francis, collection, 81
Drawing-book, Robert's, 7
"Dream, The", Blake's, 88
Druid grove, Robert Blake's, 10
Druid Symbolism, Blake's, 175
Dunhill, Sir Thomas, 155
Dürer, Albrecht, Blake's opinion of, 78
    illustrations by, 169

Edward III, drawing of, 42
Edwards, Francis, bookseller, 35,
    65 n.
Edwards, Richard, publisher, 59, 60,
    62, 64
Edwards, Thomas, of Halifax, 64
Egner, Arthur F., collection, 115
Egremont, Earl of, 141
Eleanor, Queen, drawing of, 42
Elihu, in *Job*, 147, 148, 151
Ellis, E. J., *The Real Blake*, 133
Ellis, E. J., and Yeats, W. B., 19
Ellis, F. S., 18
Ellis and Scrutton, 18

Emendations, Rossetti's, 18, 31
Emerson, Frances White, 19, 20, 65
Emery, John J., collection, 35
Encyclopaedia Britannica, article in, 196
Enoch, Blake's lithograph of, 122
"Entombment, The", Blake's, 196
Europe, Blake's, 15
Evans, Frederic H., reproductions
    by, 166
"Everlasting Gospel, The", 16, 18
Everyman Library, Dent's, xi
Examiner, The, Hunt's, 79, 86
Exchange Alley, 50-54
Excursion, Wordsworth's, 103
Ezekiel, Blake's painting of, 120

Faber Gallery, The, 198
"Fair Elenor", *Poetical Sketches*, 28, 33
Farington, Joseph, diary, 59
Felpham, Blake at, 15
Figgis, Darrell, 194
Fitzwilliam Museum, Cambridge, 81,
    118, 127, 134, 137, 144, 165
    copper-plates in, 109
    Jerusalem in, 111
Flaxman, Anna, 29, 33, 35
    present to, 64
Flaxman, John, 23-5, 29, 38, 50, 139
    Letter to the Committee, 25
    Wedgwood Catalogue, 70
Fogg Art Museum, *Job* illustrations,
    125
    Young's *Night Thoughts*, xii, 65 n.
Forget-me-not, 186
Forman, H. Buxton, 10, 37, 114
Fountain Court, Strand, 119
French Revolution, Blake's, 69
Frick Collection, New York, 173,
    183
Friendship, Blake's aphorisms on, 113
Friendship's Offering, 186
Frye, Northrop, *Fearful Symmetry*,
    xi, 199
Fuseli, Henry, 47, 50, 59, 60, 63
    "Fertilization of Egypt", 67
    and Haydon, 100

INDEX

INDEX

INDEX

INDEX

Royal Academy, donation to Blake, 119, 143
 library, 83
Rubens, Blake's opinion of, 76, 78
Ruskin, John, and MSS., 114
Russell, A. G. B., *Engravings of Blake*, 50, 122

Sadler's Wells Ballet, 155
St. Paul's Cathedral, symbolism of, 175
Saintsbury, Professor, 30
Salviati, drawing by, 46
Sampson, John, 19, 29, 30, 33
"Samson", Blake's, 30
Samson Agonistes, Milton's, 170
Satan's Trinity, 152
Savoy Hill, *Job* music broadcast from, 154
Scott, David, illustrations by, 168
Scott, Sir Walter, Blake compared with, 103
 contribution by, 187
Scott of Amwell, *Poetical Works*, 26
Serpents, engraving of, 43, 44
Severn, Arthur, 114
Shepherd, R. H., editor, 35
Shields, Frederick, 11, 66
Shury, D. N., printer, 80
Slough of Despond, the, 175
Smart, Christopher, 187
Smirke, R., opinion of Blake, 60
Smith, George C., jr., collection, 35, 115
Smith, John Thomas, 5, 7
 Nollekens and his Times, 23
Smith, William, collection, 80
"Song", *Poetical Sketches*, 33
Song of Los, Blake's, 11
Songs, Blake's, copper-plates for, 107
Songs of Experience, Blake's, 15
Sons of the Morning, origin of, 44, 124
 and Coleridge, 100
 pencil drawing of, 148
Southey, Robert, and Blake's Exhibition, 76, 87
 and *Descriptive Catalogue*, 83

Southey, Robert (*contd.*)—
 and Hayley's *Ballads*, 89
 and *Jerusalem*, 90, 92
 emendation by, 31
 The Doctor, 92
Spearman, Sir Alexander, collection, 9
Spencer, W. T., bookseller, 130
Spiral Press, the, 197
Stationers' Company records, 41
Stirling, General Archibald, 37, 117
Stirling, Lt.-Col. William, collection, 82, 117
Stirling Maxwell, Sir John, collection, 77, 82
Stirling Maxwell, Sir William, collection, 77, 82
Story, A. T., *Life of Linnell*, 135, 137, 144
Stothard, Thomas, 9, 26, 48, 50
Strang, William, illustrations by, 169
"Sweeping the Interpreter's House", Blake's, 171
Swinburne, A. C., *Critical Essay*, 18
 transcript by, 20
Symbolism, Blake's, 6, 44, 85, 110, 146, 149, 175, 178, 181
Symmetry, Blake's, 149, 151

Tate Gallery, 115, 119
Tatham, C. H., 143
Tatham, Frederick, 3, 4, 10, 107, 111, 114, 130, 143
 given *Descriptive Catalogue*, 80, 83
 Life of Blake, 117
Taylor, Josiah, and *Job*, 143
Temple of Flora, Thornton's, 187
There is no Natural Religion, Blake's, 56
Thomas, C. W., of Wisconsin, 68
Thompson, John, wood-engraving by, 158
Thornton, Dr. R. J., 157 ff., 186 ff.
Thornton, Miss, illustrations by, 187
Thoron, Mrs., collection, 116
Thurston, John, designs by, 158
Tilloch, Alexander, testimonial to, 55

INDEX

THE PLATES

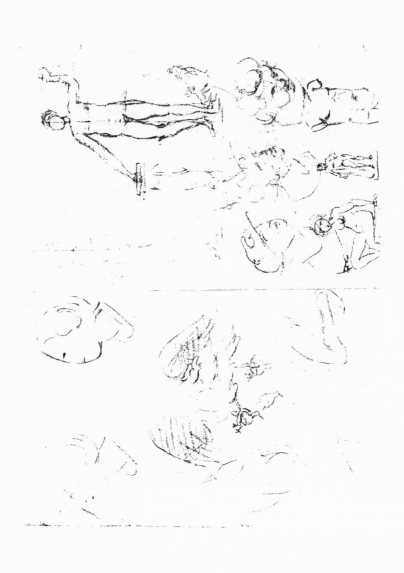

And take Revenge at the last say Joy in applied & shed in prayer
This Congenial ... ...
And a ... up of ... time
One that which was of woman born
In the absence of the Moon
When the soul fell into sleep
And unhappily would it weep
Shooting out against the light
Spirits of a dead by night
... upon th' own dark Fortune
In World which is self Contradiction
Humility is only doubt
And sees the Sun a Moon blotted out
... over with thorns & thorny
The hurried soul & all its gems
This ... the wisdom of the soul
... the ... some ... is ...
And leads you to Believe a Lie
When your see with, not thro the Eye
That was born in a night to perish in a night
When the soul slept in the beams & light — 78 lines

I never will Pray for the World
Once ... when ... in ...
I wish to take with me a Bodily Pardon

Was Jesus Chaste or did Li. ...

I'm sure this ... will not Do:
Either for Englishman or Jew

23 May 1810 from the Word of God

A Man who himself does all these & with all the Cares of Nature is fit for a Model before him & to Copy that & not as to make of a deception and to say then if any of these add lines to our Creation & the Art can do it worthy of admiration to any body of Mortals say who can not do this that man able has eyes and ears — men of patience cannot do this merely — & this Art can do it glorious — is a Nature to produce and undergo the agonies ...

No Man of Sense can think that an Imitation of the Objects of Nature in The Art of Painting & that such Imitation which any one may easily perform is worthy of Notice much less that such an Art should be the Glory & Pride of a Nation ~~and that to men did they think~~ the Italians laugh at English Connoisseurs who are most of them such silly Fellows as to believe this

London

I wander thro' each dirty street
Near where the dirty Thames does flow
And see in every face I meet
Marks of weakness marks of woe

In every cry of every man
In every infants cry of fear
In every voice in every ban
The german forged [links] I hear

How the chimney sweepers cry
[Blackens o'er] the [churches] walls [every blackning]
And the hapless soldier's sigh
Runs in blood down palace walls

But most [the midnight harlots curse]

I laughed in the dark
In the silent night
[I am] [murmured] my fears
And I felt delight

In the morning I went
Be way in morn
To seek for new joy
But I met with scorn

Sonobodaddy

Why [should] I care [for] the men of thames
Why darkness & obscurity
[In] all thy [words] [we] [hays]
[That] sang [could] the [Pent] [Bow] [bone]
The [early] [serpents] sang

The [modest] [fearful] [rose] puts forth a thorn
The [humble] [coward] sheep a threatning horn
While the lilly white shall in love delight
And [nor] a thorn nor a threat stain her beauty bright

Abstinence

When the [voices] of children [are heard on the green]
And whispers [joy in the dale]
dark [Arise] [come] [home] [my children] the [sun] is gone down
and the dews of [night] arise
Your [spring] & your [day] are [wasted] in play
And your winter & night in disguise

Are not the [joys] of morning sweeter
Than the [joys] of night
And are the [vigorous] joys of youth
Ashamed of the light

Let age & sickness silent [rob]
The [vineyards] in the night
But those who burn with [youth & pride]
[Pluck] fruits before the light

[The Tyger]

Tyger Tyger burning bright
In the forests of the night
What immortal [hand] or eye
[Dare] [frame] thy fearful symmetry

[Burnt] in [distant] deeps or skies
[The] [cruel] fire of thine eyes
On what wings dare he aspire
What the hand dare seize the fire

And what [shoulder] & what art
Could twist the [sinews] of thy heart
And when thy heart began to beat
What dread hand & what dread feet

What the [hammer] what the [chain]
In what furnace was thy brain
What the [anvil] what the [grasp]
[Dare] its deadly terrors clasp

Tyger Tyger burning bright
In the forests of the night
What immortal hand & eye
Dare frame thy fearful symmetry

(15)

MAD SONG.

THE wild winds weep,
    And the night is a-cold;
Come hither, Sleep,
    And my griefs unfold :
But lo! the morning peeps
    Over the eastern steeps,
And the ruftling beds of dawn
The earth do fcorn.

Lo! to the vault
    Of paved heaven,
With forrow fraught
    My notes are driven :
They ftrike the ear of night,
    Make weep the eyes of day ;
They make mad the roaring winds,
    And with tempefts play.

Like a fiend in a cloud
    With howling woe,
After night I do croud,
    And with night will go ;
I turn my back to the eaft,
From whence comforts have increas'd ;
For light doth feize my brain
With frantic pain.

                    SONG.

DEUS   *LUNUS.*   **OPHIS** et **OVUM**
MUNDANUM.

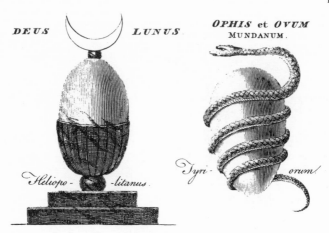

Héliopo - - -litanus.   *Tyri - - -orum.*

Tauro-Menes, et
Tauro-Menes Siculus.   *Meno-Taurus.*
Al Arhæus.

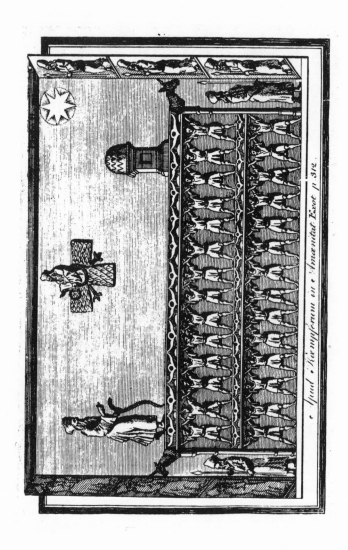

Apud Kæmpferum in Amœnitat Exot. p. 312.

12

Portrait of Edward III. from his Monument.

(10)

Sweet Harmonist! and Beautiful as sweet!
And young as beautiful! and Soft, as young!
And Gay as soft! and Innocent as gay!
And Happy (if aught Happy *here*) as Good!
For Fortune fond had built her nest on High:
Like Birds quite exquisite of Note and Plume,
Transfixt by *Fate* (who loves a lofty Mark)
How from the Summit of the Grove she fell,
And left it Unharmonious? All its Charm
Extinguisht in the Wonders of her Song!
Her Song still vibrates in my ravisht Ear,
Still melting There, and with voluptuous Pain
(O to forget her!) trilling thro' my Heart!

   Song, beauty, youth, love, virtue, joy! this Group
Of bright Ideas, Flowers of Paradise
As yet unforfeit! in one blaze we bind,
Kneel, and present it to the Skies; as All
We guess of Heaven: And these were all her Own:
                      And

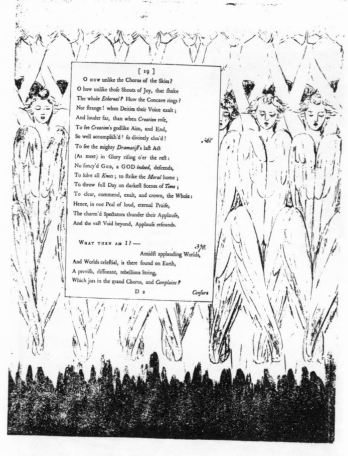

[19]

O HOW unlike the Chorus of the Skies?
O how unlike those Shouts of Joy, that shake
The whole *Ethereal*? How the Concave rings?
Nor strange! when Deities their Voice exalt ;
And louder far, than when *Creation* rose,
To see *Creation*'s godlike Aim, and End,
So well accomplish'd ! so divinely clos'd !
To see the mighty *Dramatist*'s last Act
(As meet) in Glory rising o'er the rest :
No fancy'd God, a GOD *indeed*, descends,
To solve all *Knots* ; to strike the *Moral* home ;
To throw full Day on darkest Scenes of *Time* ;
To clear, commend, exalt, and crown, the Whole :
Hence, in one Peal of loud, eternal Praise,
The charm'd Spectators thunder their Applause,
And the vast Void beyond, Applause refounds.

WHAT THEN AM I ? ——   *370.*
                    Amidst applauding Worlds,
And Worlds celestial, is there found on Earth,
A peevish, dissonant, rebellious String,
Which jars in the grand Chorus, and *Complains* ?

                    D 2   *Censure*

[40]

" And Fruits promiscuous, ever-teeming *Earth*,   700.

" That Man may languish in luxurious Scenes,

" And in an *Eden* mourn his with'ring Joys?

" Claim Earth and Skies Man's Admiration, due

" For *such* Delights ! Blest Animals ! too Wise

" To *wonder* ; and too Happy to *complain !*

" Ou r *Doom decreed* demands a mournful Scene ;

" Why not a Dungeon dark, for the *Condemn'd ?*

" Why not the Dragon's subterranean Den,

" For Man to howl in ? Why not his Abode,

" Of the same dismal Colour with his Fate?

" A *Thebes*, a *Babylon*, at vast Expence

" Of Time, Toil, Treasure, Art, for Owls and Adders,

" As congruous, as, for Man, this lofty Dome,

" Which prompts proud Thought, and kindles high Desire,

" If from her humble Chamber in the Dust,

" While proud Thought swells, and high Desire inflames,

" The poor *Worm* calls us for her Inmates there ;

" And, round us, *Death*'s inexorable Hand

" Draws the dark Curtain close; undrawn no more.

                     " *Undrawn*

[42]

Of Matter, never dignify'd with Life,
Here lie proud Rationals; The Sons of Heav'n!
The Lords of Earth! The Property of Worms!
Beings of Yesterday, and no To-morrow!
Who liv'd in Terror, and in Pangs expir'd!
All gone to rot in Chaos; or, to make
Their happy Transit into Blocks, or Brutes,
Nor longer soully their CREATOR'S *Name.*

LORENZO! hear, pause, ponder, and pronounce.
Just is this History? If *such* is Man,
Mankind's Historian, tho' Divine, might weep.
And dares LORENZO smile?—I know thee Proud;
For once let Pride befriend thee; Pride looks pale
At such a Scene, and sighs for something more.
Amid thy Boasts, Presumptions, and Displays,
And art Thou then a Shadow? Less than Shade?
A Nothing? Less than Nothing? To *have* been,
And *not to be*, is lower than Unborn.
Art thou *ambitious?* Why then make the Worm
Thine Equal? Runs thy Taste of *Pleasure* high?
Why patronize sure Death of ev'ry Joy?

Charm

The Portland Vase.

WEDGWOOD

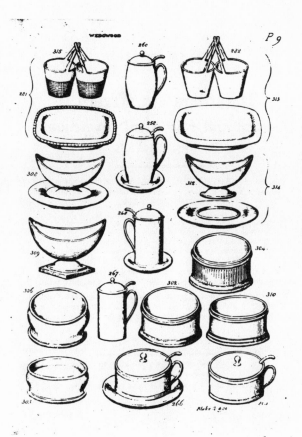

EXHIBITION

OF

Paintings in Fresco,

Poetical and Historical Inventions,

By. Wm. BLAKE.

The Ancient Britons—Three Ancient Britons overthrowing the Army of armed Romans; the Figures full as large as Life—From the Welch Triades.

In the last Battle that Arthur fought, the most Beautiful was one
That return'd, and the most Strong another: with them also return'd
The most Ugly, and no other beside return'd from the bloody Field.

The most Beautiful, the Roman Warriors trembled before and worshipped:
The most Strong, they melted before him and dissolved in his presence:
The most Ugly they fled with outcries and contortion of their Limbs.

The Canterbury Pilgrims from *Chaucer*—a cabinet Picture in Fresco—Thirty Figures on Horse-back, in a brilliant Morning Scene.

Two Pictures, representing grand Apotheoses of Nelson and Pitt, with variety of cabinet Pictures, unchangeable and permanent in Fresco, and Drawings for Public Inspection and for Sale by Private Contract, at

No. 28, *Corner of* BROAD STREET, *Golden-Square.*

"*Fit Audience find tho' few*" Milton.

Admittance 2s. 6d. each Person, a discriptive Catalogue included.

Watts & Co. Printers, Southmolton St.

A DESCRIPTIVE CATALOGUE

OF

BLAKE's EXHIBITION,

At No. 28, Corner of

BROAD-STREET,

GOLDEN-SQUARE.

THE grand Style of Art restored ; in FRESCO, or Water-colour Painting, and England protected from the too just imputation of being the Seat and Protectress of bad (that is blotting and blurring) Art.

In this Exhibition will be seen real Art, as it was left us by *Raphael* and *Albert Durer*, *Michael Angelo*, and *Julio Romano;* stripped from the Ignorances of *Rubens* and *Rembrandt*, *Titian* and *Correggio* ;

BY WILLIAM BLAKE.

The Descriptive Catalogue, Price 2s 6d. containing Mr B's Opinions and Determinations on Art, very necessary to be known by Artists and Connoisseurs of all Ranks Every Purchaser of a Catalogue will be entitled, at the time of purchase, to view the Exhibition.

These Original Conceptions on Art, by an Original Artist, are Sold only at the Corner of BROAD STREET.

Admittance to the Exhibition 1 *Shilling ; an Index to the Catalogue gratis.*

Printed by Watts & Bridgewater, Southmolton-street.

A
DESCRIPTIVE CATALOGUE

OF

PICTURES,

Poetical and Historical Inventions,

PAINTED BY

WILLIAM BLAKE,

IN

WATER COLOURS,

BEING THE ANCIENT METHOD OF

FRESCO PAINTING RESTORED:

AND

DRAWINGS,

FOR PUBLIC INSPECTION,

AND FOR

Sale by Private Contract,

at N 28 Corner of Broad Street Golden Square

LONDON:

Printed by. D. N. SHURY, 7, Berwick-Street, Soho,
for J. BLAKE, 28, Broad-Street, Golden-Square.

1809.

The Dog

Pub.d June 18. 1804 by R. Phillips N.6. Bridge Street Black Friars

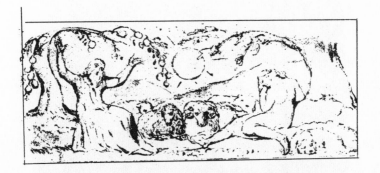

40

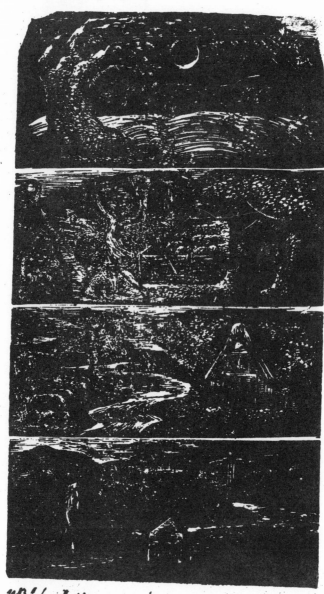

W Blake fecit

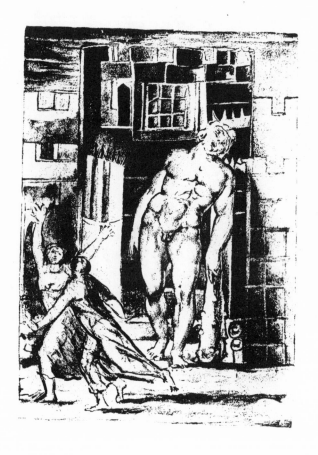

The Hiding of Moses